新编中文课外阅读丛书
TALES AND TRADITIONS

VOLUME 1   FABLES, MYTHS, AND HISTORICAL FIGURES
寓言、神话与名人故事
FOR ADVANCED BEGINNERS

SECOND EDITION

萧云   肖慧   王莹
YUN XIAO   HUI XIAO   YING WANG

CHENG & TSUI

BOSTON

CHENG & TSUI

Copyright ©2016, 2008
Cheng & Tsui Company, Inc.
Second Edition

22 21 20 19 18   2 3 4 5 6

Cheng & Tsui Company, Inc.
25 West Street
Boston, MA 02111-1213 USA
chengtsui.co
Phone (617) 988-2400 / (800) 554-1963
Fax (617) 426-3669

ISBN 978-1-62291-115-8

Printed in the United States of America

The Library of Congress has catalogued the first edition as:

Xiao, Yun.

Tales & traditions and other essays : for beginning students /
Yun Xiao, Hui Xiao, Ying Wang.
p. cm. — (Readings in Chinese literature series =
[Xin bian Zhong wen ke wai yue du cong shu] ; vol. 1)
Includes index.
ISBN 978-0-88727-534-0 [First Edition]

1. Chinese language—Textbooks for foreign speakers—
English. 2. Fables, Chinese—Adaptations.

I. Xiao, Hui. II. Wang, Ying. III. Title.

PL1129.E5X52 2007
495.1'86421—dc22
2007062024

Credits:
Illustrations by Xin Shen 沈歆
Cover image © iBird - Shutterstock

CONTENTS

目录
目錄

III 神话故事 / 神話故事
MYTHS AND FANTASIES **125**

PREFACE TO THE SECOND EDITION

Chinese is the language of the country with the largest population in the world, and in the United States, Chinese is the language of the second-largest group of non-English speakers, after only Spanish. To date, although a number of comprehensive Chinese textbooks are currently available in the United States, interesting and informative pleasure-reading materials specifically designed for Chinese are scarce at all levels. Learners and instructors of Chinese as a foreign language (CFL) have longed for such materials, and as the first AP® Chinese Language and Culture exam was offered in 2007, the need for quality readings that familiarize students with expressions essential to understanding Chinese culture is now greater than ever.

Tales and Traditions 《新编中文课外阅读丛书》/《新編中文課外閱讀叢書》 was created to meet the need for supplementary reading materials for Chinese language learners. Foreign language acquisition research has shown that extensive pleasure reading, in which students read large quantities of level-appropriate books and materials, is essential to attaining fluency in a foreign language. Pleasure reading not only improves students' reading skills, speed, and language proficiency, but also leads them to lifelong fluency and enjoyment of reading in the target language. This series presents stories and anecdotes that are a part of the Chinese literary canon and essential for cultural fluency: sayings from classical philosophers, folk tales, legends, excerpts from great works of literature, and more.

Volume 1 is designed for students who have finished the beginning level of Chinese study. Its three chapters, organized by theme, include ten Chinese literary quotations and fables; seven anecdotes from well-known figures such as Confucius and Sima Guang; and six mythological stories and fantasies. Material within each theme increases in difficulty, but students and teachers should be able to read the selections in any order.

Each text in this series has an interesting story line, a vocabulary list, and stimulating post-text questions. The texts can be used both for individual student reading and/or for instructor-facilitated classroom reading. Using the discussion questions, teachers can engage students in comprehension checks, cross-cultural comparisons, real-life reflections, and extended research. Students may also enjoy acting out the stories (see the "Teaching Note" at the end of this Preface for more information). Teachers will find the texts easy to use and an essential tool to improve learners' presentation skills. The stories will help students gain literacy and familiarity with Chinese written texts that are at the heart of Chinese culture. This focus on reading comprehension and cultural knowledge makes *Tales & Traditions* an excellent companion for students who are preparing for the AP® Chinese Language and Culture exam, or other standardized tests.

An appendix of *pinyin*-annotated texts is included in Volume 1 for students who struggle with character recognition, and a comprehensive index of all vocabulary words, arranged in alphabetical order by *pinyin*, will help students review and look up unfamiliar words. Proper nouns that appear in the stories are underlined, so that students can easily recognize and identify them.

About the *Tales & Traditions* Series

Differentiated in the use of characters, phrases, sentence patterns, and discourse features, the series consists of four volumes for advanced-beginning, intermediate, low advanced, and advanced levels. All stories are adapted to a level appropriate for learners of Chinese. Each level includes a variety of genres, such as myths, legends, classical and popular short stories, fables, Tang/Song poems, satirical and amusing essays and stories, and excerpts of well-known literature. Texts from beginning to advanced levels are all illustrated. Authentic texts, vocabulary words, and sentence patterns were adapted to keep the stories level-appropriate, while maintaining their originality.

In each volume, vocabulary words, forms of usage, idioms, and phrases are selected according to their frequency of use and expository requirements. Vocabulary glossing is cumulative, so that if a word is glossed in the first story, it will not be glossed again in later stories. Students should focus on reading for comprehension, rather than being able to recognize each and every character. For students' ease of vocabulary reference, however, an appendix of *pinyin* texts is included in Volume 1 so that students can quickly check the pronunciation of a word and look it up in the glossary or in a dictionary.

To adapt these stories and compile vocabulary lists, we used three main sources: *Xiandai Hanyu Pinlu Cidian* (現代漢語頻率詞典) (1986), *Hanyu Shuiping Dengji Biaozhun he Dengji Dagang* (漢語水平等級標準和等級大綱) (1988), and *Far East 3000 Chinese Character Dictionary* (遠東漢字三千字典) (2003). Words and phrases used at the beginning, intermediate, and advanced levels are selected in accordance with the 甲 乙 丙 levels specified in 漢語水平等級標準和等級大綱. The length of the texts gradually increases as the

Preface to the Second Edition

academic level advances, from 150 to 1,000 characters per text for the beginning and intermediate levels, and from 500 to 2,000 characters per text for the advanced levels. For the first two levels, we selected the 1,500 most frequently used words listed in 現代漢語頻率詞典 and expanded to 3,500 words for the advanced levels.

As globalization, multiculturalism, and multilingualism change the way people interact with each other around the globe, a high level of Chinese language proficiency has become an important qualification for individuals in the United States and other English-speaking countries to gain a competitive advantage in academics, business, and other areas. We hope this series of stories will help students become fluent readers and speakers of Chinese, as well as global citizens with a multicultural perspective.

What's New in the Second Edition?

Discussion questions in the new edition of *Tales and Traditions* have been revised to better prepare students for the reading comprehension questions on the AP® Exam in Chinese Language and Culture. The layout of the text is now easier to read. Background information about historical figures has been added before related texts.

TEACHING NOTE

For teachers and students who are using this book as supplementary reading for a Chinese course, we have provided questions to stimulate class discussions of the stories. In addition, students can be asked to retell the stories in their own words when class time allows. For extra speaking practice, students may enjoy acting out the stories in small groups. Each group selects a story, writes speaking lines, and assigns roles. A special day or two can be set aside at mid-term or semester's end for performance of the plays.

ABBREVIATIONS OF PARTS OF SPEECH

Part of Speech	Definition
adj.	*Adjective*
adv.	*Adverb*
conj.	*Conjunction*
mw.	*Measure word*
n.	*Noun*
on.	*Onomatopoeic word*
part.	*Particle*
pn.	*Proper noun*
v.	*Verb*
vc.	*Verb plus complement*
vo.	*Verb plus object*

I

FABLES AND LITERARY QUOTATIONS

第一章 寓言典故
第一章 寓言典故

1

PULLING SEEDLINGS UP TO HELP THEM GROW

拔苗助长₁

拔苗助長₁

Bá miáo zhù zhǎng

从前，有一个农民₂住在一个小村子₃里。他每天早上很早起床到地里去工作，晚上很晚才回家。

　　一年春天，他在地里下了种子₄，不久就长出了禾苗₅。他非常高兴，天天给禾苗浇水₆，希望它们快快长高。他还每天都用一把尺子去量₇这些禾苗，看看它们长高了多少。十几天过去了，他觉得禾苗长得太慢了，很着急₈。他想："怎样才能让这些禾苗长得快一点呢？"

　　他想啊想啊，想出了一个办法："如果我把这些禾苗都往上拔高一点儿，它们不就都长高了吗？"他很快跑₉到地里，把所有的禾苗都拔高了一点儿。

　　他拔到半夜才回家。虽然很累₁₀，但是很高兴。他告诉儿子说："我今天帮助地里的禾苗长高了！"他的儿子到地里一看，却发现₁₁所有的禾苗都死₁₂了。

從前，有一個農民₂住在一個小村子₃裡。他每天早上很早起床到地裡去工作，晚上很晚才回家。

一年春天，他在地裡下了種子₄，不久就長出了禾苗₅。他非常高興，天天給禾苗澆水₆，希望它們快快長高。他還每天都用一把尺子去量₇這些禾苗，看看它們長高了多少。十幾天過去了，他覺得禾苗長得太慢了，很著急₈。他想：“怎樣才能讓這些禾苗長得快一點呢？”

他想啊想啊，想出了一個辦法：“如果我把這些禾苗都往上拔高一點兒，它們不就都長高了嗎？”他很快跑₉到地裡，把所有的禾苗都拔高了一點兒。

他拔到半夜才回家。雖然很累₁₀，但是很高興。他告訴兒子說：“我今天幫助地裡的禾苗長高了！”他的兒子到地裡一看，卻發現₁₁所有的禾苗都死₁₂了。

VOCABULARY LIST

SIMPLIFIED CHARACTERS	TRADITIONAL CHARACTERS	*PINYIN*	PART OF SPEECH	ENGLISH DEFINITION
1. 拔	拔	bá	v.	to pull
苗	苗	miáo	n.	seedling; shoot
助	助	zhù	v.	to help
长	長	zhǎng	v.	to grow
2. 农民	農民	nóngmín	n.	farmer
3. 村子	村子	cūnzi	n.	village
4. 种子	種子	zhǒngzi	n.	seeds
5. 禾苗	禾苗	hémiáo	n	shoots of grain
6. 浇水	澆水	jiāoshǔi	vo.	to give water to plants
7. 量	量	liáng	v.	to measure
8. 着急	著急	zháojí	adj.	worry
9. 跑	跑	pǎo	v.	to run
10. 累	累	lèi	adj.	tired
11. 发现	發現	fāxiàn	v.	to discover
12. 死	死	sǐ	v.	to die or to become withered

---

*Note: All vocabulary words in this book are numbered within the texts for easy reference.

Reading Comprehension

1. What did the farmer do in the spring?

    A. He moved to a small village.

    B. He worked at home all day.

    C. He planted some seeds in the field.

    D. He bought some grain.

2. What did the farmer do first to help his plants grow faster?

    A. He watered them daily.

    B. He watered them every other day.

    C. He pulled them up.

    D. He measured them with a ruler.

3. What did he find and how did he feel several days later?

    A. He found that the plants grew quickly and was enthusiastic.

    B. He found that the plants grew quickly and was satisfied.

    C. He found that the plants grew slowly and was disappointed.

    D. He found that the plants grew slowly and was impatient.

4. After thinking things over, the farmer decided to

    A. work extra hard by getting up early in the morning and going home late at night.

    B. move from the village to the field.

    C. pull all the plants up a little bit.

    D. ask his son for help.

5. How did he feel when he came home at midnight?

   A.   Happy and exhausted

   B.   Happy and energetic

   C.   Sad and discouraged

   D.   Sad and hungry

6. What did the farmer's son discover when he went to the field?

   A.   The plants were taller.

   B.   The plants were dead.

   C.   The plants were extremely tall.

   D.   The plants were not there.

7. Which sentence best describes the moral of this story?

   A.   One should not interfere with nature.

   B.   It is better to start early than rush at the end.

   C.   A gentle approach will produce better results.

   D.   It is better to wait patiently than to act rashly.

Discussion

1. Do you know any idioms or proverbs from another culture that have a similar message?

2. Describe a situation in which it would be appropriate to use this idiom.

2

SITTING BY A STUMP TO WAIT FOR A CARELESS HARE

守株待兔₁
守株待兔₁

Shǒu zhū dài tù

很久以前，有一个农民在很远的地方种了一块地。地的旁边有一个树桩，树桩旁边长满了野草，如果不仔细看的话，就看不出里面有一个树桩。有时这个农民累了，就坐在树桩上休息。

有一天，这个农民正在工作，一只野兔飞一样地从远处跑过来。这只野兔因为跑得太快，没有看到野草里的树桩，一头撞在树桩上，就昏过去了。农民看见了，马上拾起野兔。他非常高兴，心里想："要是每天都有一只野兔从这里跑过，并且撞在这个树桩上，那我为什么还要辛辛苦苦地工作呢？"

从这天以后，这个农民再也不去工作了。他每天早上都来到地里，坐在离树桩不远的地方等着，希望还会有野兔跑过来撞在那儿。

农夫等啊，等啊，一天、两天、三天，很多天过去了，他的地里已经长满了野草。虽然还常有野兔从地边跑过，可是没有一只正好撞在那个树桩上。最后，他连吃饭的钱都没有了，成了人们的笑话。

Why no ba?

很久以前，有一個農民在很遠的地方種了一塊[2]地。地的旁邊有一個樹樁[3]，樹樁旁邊長滿了野草[4]，如果不仔細[5]看的話，就看不出裡面有一個樹樁。有時這個農民累了，就坐在樹樁上休息[6]。

有一天，這個農民正在工作，一隻野兔飛一樣地從遠處跑過來。這隻野兔因為跑得太快，沒有看到野草裡的樹樁，一頭撞[7]在樹樁上，就昏[8]過去了。農民看見了，馬上拾[9]起野兔。他非常高興，心裡想："要是每天都有一隻野兔從這裏跑過，並且[10]撞在這個樹樁上，那我為什麼還要辛辛苦苦[11]地工作呢？"

從這天以後，這個農民再也不去工作了。他每天早上都來到地裡，坐在離樹樁不遠的地方等著，希望還會有野兔跑過來撞在那兒。

農夫等啊，等啊，一天、兩天、三天，很多天過去了，他的地裡已經長滿了野草。雖然還常有野兔從地邊跑過，可是沒有一隻正好撞在那個樹樁上。最後，他連吃飯的錢都沒有了，成了人們的笑話[12]。

SIMPLIFIED CHARACTERS	TRADITIONAL CHARACTERS	*PINYIN*	PART OF SPEECH	ENGLISH DEFINITION
1. 守	守	shǒu	v.	to stay around
株	株	zhū	n.	tree stump
待	待	dài	v.	to wait
兔	兔	tù	n.	hare, rabbit
2. 块	塊	kuài	mw.	measure word for a piece, lump, chunk
3. 树桩	樹樁	shùzhuāng	n.	tree stump
4. 野草	野草	yěcǎo	n.	weeds, wild grass
5. 仔细	仔細	zǐxì	n.	carefully
6. 休息	休息	xīuxi	v.	to rest
7. 撞	撞	zhuàng	v.	to collide
8. 昏	昏	hūn	v.	to faint
9. 拾	拾	shí	v.	to pick up
10. 并且	並且	bìngqiě	conj.	also
11. 辛辛苦苦	辛辛苦苦	xīnxīnkǔkǔ	adj.	painstaking
12. 笑话	笑話	xiàohuà	n.	joke, laughingstock

QUESTIONS

Reading Comprehension

1. What was the tree stump surrounded by?

   A. Shoots of grain

   B. Wild grass

   C. Flowers

   D. Fruit trees

2. Where did the farmer take a break when he got tired?

   A. In the field.

   B. On the wild grass.

   C. Under a tree.

   D. On the tree stump.

3. What happened to the hare?

   A. It fell into a hole.

   B. It ran into the stump.

   C. It could not see the farmer in the grass and was caught.

   D. It stopped near the stump and was caught.

4. What did the farmer do to the hare?

   A. He saved the hare.

   B. He raised the hare.

   C. He picked up the hare.

   D. He ignored the hare.

5. What best explains why the farmer stopped working?

   A. He liked the taste of rabbit.

   B. He thought catching rabbits would get him more money than working in the fields.

   C. He was too old and tired to continue working in the fields.

   D. He thought waiting for rabbits would be easier than working in the fields.

6. How long did the farmer wait by the stump?

   A. Two days

   B. Three days

   C. Several days

   D. Several hours

7. Which sentence best describes the moral of this story?

   A. It is better to wait patiently than to act rashly.

   B. Many tasks are far more difficult than they appear to be to outsiders.

   C. One should not rely on luck rather than on hard work.

   D. Take advantage of each opportunity when it appears.

Discussion

1. If you were the farmer, what would you do at the end of the story? Why?

2. Do you know any idioms or proverbs from another culture that have a similar message?

3. Describe a situation in which it would be appropriate to use this idiom.

3

DRAWING A SNAKE AND ADDING FEET

画蛇添足₁

畫蛇添足₁

Huà shé tiān zú

很久以前，有一个富人₂，家里有很多仆人₃。有一天，*他给了他们一瓶酒，这酒好香₄啊！可是，只有一瓶，仆人却有十几个。怎么办呢？这时，有一个仆人说："酒太少了，只够一个人喝，让我们来一场₅比赛₆吧。我们每个人都用笔在地上画一条蛇，谁先画好，这瓶酒就让他一个人喝，好不好？"大家都说"好。"

然后，他们都拿好了笔，一、二、三，开始！大家同时在地上画起蛇来。有一个人很快就画好了。他看见其他的人还在画着，就说："你们画得真慢！你们看，我早就画完了！这酒是我的了。"他把酒拿过来，又看了看其他的人，笑着说："你们还在画呢，那我再给我的蛇画四只脚₇吧！"他一边说，一边在画好的蛇上又画了四只脚。

可是，还没等他把脚画好，第二个人已经画完了。这个人马上从他手里把酒抢₈过来，说："我们比赛画蛇，可是蛇没有脚啊！现在你却给它画上了脚，那还能叫蛇吗？现在我是第一个画完蛇的人了，所以这瓶酒应该是我的！"说完他就开始喝起来。第一个画完蛇的人非常生气₉，可是一句话也说不出来，因为这是他自己的过错₁₀啊！

16　　　　　　　　　　　　画蛇添足 | SIMPLIFIED

很久以前，有一個富人[2]，家裡有很多僕人[3]。有一天，他給了他們一瓶酒。這酒好香[4]啊！可是，只有一瓶，僕人卻有十幾個。怎麼辦呢？這時，有一個僕人說："酒太少了，只夠一個人喝，讓我們來一場[5]比賽[6]吧。我們每個人都用筆在地上畫一條蛇，誰先畫好，這瓶酒就讓他一個人喝，好不好？"大家都說"好。"

然後，他們都拿好了筆，一、二、三，開始！大家同時在地上畫起蛇來。有一個人很快就畫好了。他看見其他的人還在畫著，就說："你們畫得真慢！你們看，我早就畫完了！這酒是我的了。"他把酒拿過來，又看了看其他的人，笑著說："你們還在畫呢，那我再給我的蛇畫四隻腳[7]吧！"他一邊說，一邊在畫好的蛇上又畫了四隻腳。

可是，還沒等他把腳畫好，第二個人已經畫完了。這個人馬上從他手裡把酒搶[8]過來，說："我們比賽畫蛇，可是蛇沒有腳啊！現在你卻給它畫上了腳，那還能叫蛇嗎？現在我是第一個畫完蛇的人了，所以這瓶酒應該是我的！"說完他就開始喝起來。第一個畫完蛇的人非常生氣[9]，可是一句話也說不出來，因為這是他自己的過錯[10]啊！

VOCABULARY LIST

SIMPLIFIED CHARACTERS	TRADITIONAL CHARACTERS	*PINYIN*	PART OF SPEECH	ENGLISH DEFINITION
1. 画	畫	huà	v.	to draw
蛇	蛇	shé	n.	snake
添	添	tiān	v.	to add
足	足	zú	n.	feet
2. 富人	富人	fùrén	n.	rich person
3. 仆人	僕人	púrén	n.	servant
4. 香	香	xiāng	adj.	fragrant, sweet-smelling
5. 场	場	chǎng	mw.	measure word for happenings or occurrences
6. 比赛	比賽	bǐsài	v.	competition
7. 脚	腳	jiǎo	n.	foot
8. 抢	搶	qiǎng	v.	to grab
9. 生气	生氣	shēngqì	adj.	angry
10. 过错	過錯	guòcuò	n.	fault, mistake

QUESTIONS

Reading Comprehension

1. How many servants are in the family?

    A. Less than ten

    B. Ten to twenty

    C. Twenty to thirty

    D. More than thirty

2. Why did the servants have a competition?

    A. To decide who the best painter was.

    B. To decide who would get to taste their master's wine.

    C. To determine what a snake looks like.

    D. To decide who would get a bottle of wine.

3. What did the servant who finished first continue to do?

    A. He finished drinking the wine.

    B. He accidentally dropped the wine.

    C. He drew feet on the snake.

    D. He hung his drawing on the wall.

4. Why did the servant who finished first lose the prize?

    A. He did not speak up after he finished.

    B. He drew on another servant's painting and was disqualified.

    C. He did not draw a snake properly.

    D. He mocked the other contestants and was disqualified.

5. When did the winner finish his painting?

   A.   While the servant who finished first was drawing feet on the snake.

   B.   After the servant who finished first drew feet on the snake.

   C.   While the servant who finished first was drinking his wine.

   D.   After the servant who finished first drank his wine.

6. According to the servant who finished first, who was at fault?

   A.   The master

   B.   The winner

   C.   All the other servants

   D.   Himself

7. Which sentence best describes the moral of this story?

   A.   You can ruin something by overdoing it.

   B.   Humility will be rewarded; arrogance will be punished.

   C.   Preparation is key to success.

   D.   True talent is often misunderstood.

Discussion

1. Why do you think the servant who finished first did what he did?

2. Do you know any idioms or proverbs from another culture that have a similar message?

3. Describe a situation in which it would be appropriate to use this idiom.

4

MISTAKING THE REFLECTION OF A BOW FOR A SNAKE

杯 弓 蛇 影 ₁

杯 弓 蛇 影 ₁

Bēi gōng shé yǐng

中国古代有一个人叫乐广₂。乐广*有很多朋友，他最喜欢做的事情就是请他的朋友们到家里来喝酒，聊天儿。

有一天，乐广的一个好朋友到他家来了，两个人一边喝酒，一边聊天。正当他们聊得很高兴的时候，他的朋友却推开₃酒杯，说自己的肚子不舒服，然后就急急忙忙₄地回家去了。乐广觉得非常奇怪₅，很想知道为什么。

第二天，乐广到朋友家去，发现他躺

在床上，好象病得很重。乐广问："你今天怎么样？"朋友说："我生病了。"乐广问："什么病呢？"朋友说："昨天我在你家里喝酒的时候，看见一条小蛇在我的酒杯里，我觉得恶心₆，可是我还是喝下去了。我一喝下去，就觉得肚子很不舒服，回家就生病了。"

乐广想："我家的酒里怎么会有蛇呢？"回家以后，他坐在朋友

*Note: In the stories in this book, underlined words are proper nouns.

中國古代有一個人叫樂廣[2]。樂廣*有很多朋友，他最喜歡做的事情就是請他的朋友們到家裡來喝酒，聊天兒。

　　有一天，樂廣的一個好朋友到他家來了，兩個人一邊喝酒，一邊聊天。正當他們聊得很高興的時候，他的朋友卻推開[3]酒杯，說自己的肚子不舒服，然後就急急忙忙[4]地回家去了。樂廣覺得非常奇怪[5]，很想知道為什麼。

　　第二天，樂廣到朋友家去，發現他躺在床上，好象病得很重。樂廣問："你今天怎麼樣？"朋友說："我生病了。"樂廣問："什麼病呢？"朋友說："昨天我在你家裡喝酒的時候，看見一條小蛇在我的酒杯裡，我覺得噁心[6]，可是我還是喝下去了。我一喝下去，就覺得肚子很不舒服，回家就生病了。"

　　樂廣想："我家的酒裡怎麼會有蛇呢？"回家以後，他坐在朋友

的座位上，并且在面前放了一杯酒。他一看酒杯，里面真的有一条小蛇！这是怎么回事呢？<u>乐广</u>抬头一看，原来座位旁边的墙[7]上挂[8]着一张弓，那张弓的影子映[9]在酒杯里，就好象是一条小蛇。

<u>乐广</u>马上回到朋友那儿，请朋友再到自己家来。<u>乐广</u>请他坐在原来的座位上，又给他倒了一杯酒。朋友一看酒杯，吓得大叫起来："蛇！蛇！"<u>乐广</u>哈哈大笑，慢慢地站起来，把挂在墙上的弓拿掉。这时朋友再看酒杯，发现酒杯里的蛇不见了。原来酒杯里根本[10]没有小蛇！朋友的"病"一下子就好了，肚子也不疼了。

的座位上，並且在面前放了一杯酒。他一看酒杯，裡面真的有一條小蛇！這是怎麼回事呢？樂廣抬頭一看，原來座位旁邊的牆上掛[8]著一張弓，那張弓的影子映[9]在酒杯裡，就好象是一條小蛇。

樂廣馬上回到朋友那兒，請朋友再到自己家來。樂廣請他坐在原來的座位上，又給他倒了一杯酒。朋友一看酒杯，嚇得大叫起來："蛇！蛇！"樂廣哈哈大笑，慢慢地站起來，把掛在牆上的弓拿掉。這時朋友再看酒杯，發現酒杯裡的蛇不見了。原來酒杯裡根本[10]沒有小蛇！朋友的"病"一下子就好了，肚子也不疼了。

VOCABULARY LIST

	SIMPLIFIED CHARACTERS	TRADITIONAL CHARACTERS	*PINYIN*	PART OF SPEECH	ENGLISH DEFINITION
1.	杯	杯	bēi	n.	cup
	弓	弓	gōng	n.	bow
	蛇	蛇	shé	n.	snake
	影	影	yǐng	n.	reflection
2.	乐广	樂廣	Yuè Guǎng	pn.	name of a person
3.	推开	推開	tuīkāi	v.	to push away
4.	急急忙忙	急急忙忙	jíjímángmáng	adv.	in a hurry
5.	奇怪	奇怪	qíguài	adj.	strange
6.	恶心	噁心	ěxīn	v.	to feel sick
7.	墙	牆	qiáng	n.	wall
8.	挂	掛	guà	v.	to hang
9.	映	映	yìng	v.	to reflect
10.	根本	根本	gēnběn	adv.	actually

Mistaking the Reflection of a Bow for a Snake

QUESTIONS

Reading Comprehension

1. What is Yue Guang's favorite thing to do?

    A. Spending time with friends.

    B. Visiting his friends' houses.

    C. Inviting his friends to his home for drinks.

    D. Chatting with his friends and playing chess.

2. When Yue Guang and his friend were drinking and talking, why did his friend say he had to go home quickly?

    A. He had drunk too much wine.

    B. He had seen a snake in his wine cup.

    C. He had seen something strange.

    D. His stomach was unwell.

3. What was Yue Guang's friend doing when he visited him the next day?

    A. Lying on the couch.

    B. Lying on the bed.

    C. Sitting in a chair.

    D. Walking around.

4. When Yue Guang visited his friend the next day, what did his friend say had made him sick?

    A. He had drunk too much wine.

    B. He had seen a spider in his wine cup.

    C. He had seen a snake in his wine cup.

    D. He had eaten something that made him sick.

Mistaking the Reflection of a Bow for a Snake   **27**

5. How did Yue Guang's friend feel when he drank the wine?

   A. Scared

   B. Nauseous

   C. Excited

   D. Drunk

6. What was it that actually made Yue Guang's friend feel sick?

   A. A snake hanging on the wall.

   B. A rope hanging on the wall.

   C. A light hanging on the wall.

   D. A bow hanging on the wall.

7. This idiom could best be used to describe which of these situations?

   A. Someone gets out of an appointment by faking illness.

   B. A man imagines he sees tornadoes in the clouds whenever it rains.

   C. Two friends are fighting over a simple misunderstanding.

   D. Someone mistakes a stranger for one of their friends.

Discussion

1. What could explain the friend's quick recovery?

2. Do you know any idioms or proverbs from another culture that have a similar meaning?

3. Do you think this story has a "moral"? How would you describe its message?

5

SIX BLIND MEN AND AN ELEPHANT

盲人摸象₁

盲人摸象₁

Máng rén mō xiàng

在很远的地方，有一个城市[2]，那儿住着六个盲人。这六个盲人是好朋友，他们常常在一起聊天儿。有一天，他们听说有人从很远的地方带回来一只很大的动物，叫大象。因为谁都没有见过这种动物，所以大家都去看它。

这些盲人也很想知道大象是什么样子。虽然他们看不见，可是可以用手摸啊！所以他们也来到大象面前，都用手去摸一摸，然后说说它的样子。

第一个盲人摸到了大象的鼻子[3]，他说："哦，原来大象是一条圆圆[4]的、粗粗[5]的、长长的管子[6]啊！"

第二个盲人摸到了大象的耳朵[7]，他说："不对，大象是一把大扇子[8]，搧[9]起风来可凉快呢！"

第三个盲人摸到了大象的身体[10]，他说："你们都错了，大象是一堵[11]又高又大的墙！"

第四个盲人摸到了大象的腿[12]他说："你们说什么呀，大象是一根又粗又圆的大柱子[13]啊！"

第五个盲人摸到了大象的尾巴[14]，他说："你们都不对，大象只是一条长长的绳子[15]。"

第六个盲人摸到了大象的牙齿[16]，他说："我觉得大象不长也不短[17]，摸起来很光滑[18]。"

六个盲人都觉得只有自己才是对的，谁也不让谁。这时，人们笑着对他们说："你们每个人都说对了，但又没有一个人全[19]对。因为你们都只摸到了大象的一部分[20]，并没有摸到大象的全部！"

在很遠的地方，有一個城市₂，那兒住著六個盲人。這六個盲人是好朋友，他們常常在一起聊天兒。有一天，他們聽說有人從很遠的地方帶回來一隻很大的動物，叫大象。因為誰都沒有見過這種動物，所以大家都去看它。

這些盲人也很想知道大象是什麼樣子。雖然他們看不見，可是可以用手摸啊！所以他們也來到大象面前，都用手去摸一摸，然後說說它的樣子。

第一個盲人摸到了大象的鼻子₃，他說："哦，原來大象是一條圓圓₄的、粗粗₅的、長長的管子₆啊！"

第二個盲人摸到了大象的耳朵₇，他說："不對，大象是一把大扇子₈，搧₉起風來可涼快呢！"

第三個盲人摸到了大象的身體₁₀，他說："你們都錯了，大象是一堵₁₁又高又大的牆！"

第四個盲人摸到了大象的腿₁₂他說："你們說什麼呀，大象是一根又粗又圓的大柱子₁₃啊！"

第五個盲人摸到了大象的尾巴₁₄，他說："你們都不對，大象只是一條長長的繩子₁₅。"

第六個盲人摸到了大象的牙齒₁₆，他說："我覺得大象不長也不短₁₇，摸起來很光滑₁₈。"

六個盲人都覺得只有自己才是對的，誰也不讓誰。這時，人們笑著對他們說："你們每個人都說對了，但又沒有一個人全₁₉對。因為你們都只摸到了大象的一部分₂₀，並沒有摸到大象的全部！"

VOCABULARY LIST

	SIMPLIFIED CHARACTERS	TRADITIONAL CHARACTERS	*PINYIN*	PART OF SPEECH	ENGLISH DEFINITION
1.	盲人	盲人	mángrén	n.	blind person
	摸	摸	mō	v.	to touch, to feel
	象(大象)	象(大象)	xiàng	n.	elephant
2.	城市	城市	chéngshì	n.	city
3.	鼻子	鼻子	bízi	n.	nose (in this story, an elephant's trunk)
4.	圆	圓	yuán	adj.	round
5.	粗	粗	cū	adj.	thick and strong
6.	管子	管子	guǎnzi	n.	a tube
7.	耳朵	耳朵	ěrduō	n.	ear
8.	扇子	扇子	shànzi	n.	fan
9.	搧	搧	shān	v.	to wave a fan
10.	身体	身體	shēntǐ	n.	body
11.	堵	堵	dǔ	mw.	measure word for walls
12.	腿	腿	tuǐ	n.	leg
13.	柱子	柱子	zhùzi	n.	pillar
14.	尾巴	尾巴	wěibā	n.	tail
15.	绳子	繩子	shéngzi	n.	rope

	SIMPLIFIED CHARACTERS	TRADITIONAL CHARACTERS	*PINYIN*	PART OF SPEECH	ENGLISH DEFINITION
16.	牙齿	牙齒	yáchǐ	n.	teeth (elephant's tusk)
17.	短	短	duǎn	adj.	short
18.	光滑	光滑	guānghuá	adj.	smooth
19.	全	全	quán	adv.	entire
20.	部分	部分	bùfen	n.	part, portion

QUESTIONS

Reading Comprehension

1. What do the six blind men usually like to do?

   A. Play musical instruments.

   B. Go outside to bask in the sun.

   C. Have a feast.

   D. Chat with each other.

2. How many of the blind men have seen an elephant before?

   A. None

   B. One

   C. Three

   D. All

3. What did the first blind man describe the elephant as?

   A. A wall

   B. A fan

   C. A tube

   D. A rope

4. What part of the elephant did the second blind man touch?

   A. The nose

   B. The ears

   C. The tail

   D. The body

5. What part of the elephant did the fifth blind man touch?

    A. The legs

    B. The ears

    C. The tail

    D. The tusks

6. The sixth blind man describes the elephant as being very

    A. long.

    B. short.

    C. smooth.

    D. rough.

7. Which sentence best describes the moral of this story?

    A. It is better to think before you speak.

    B. Only looking at pieces will not give a good picture of the whole.

    C. Too many conflicting opinions will prevent effective action.

    D. Cooperation is more important than individual effort.

Discussion

1. Are any of the blind men incorrect?

2. Do you know any idioms or proverbs from another culture that have a similar message?

3. Describe a situation in which it would be appropriate to use this idiom.

6

SELF-CONTRADICTION

自 相 矛 盾₁
自 相 矛 盾₁

Zì xiāng máo dùn

很久以前，中国分成[2]了几个小国，这些小国常常打仗[3]。那时候，人们打仗用的武器[4]是矛和盾。矛是用来进攻[5]的，有长长的木柄[6]，木柄的一头装着锋利[7]的矛头[8]，又叫长矛。盾是用来防卫[9]的，用坚硬[10]的金属[11]做成的，打仗时用它挡住[12]身体，可以保护[13]自己不受长矛的攻击。

一天，有一个人在市场[14]上卖武器。他卖的就是矛和盾。他把矛放在一边，又把盾放在另外一边，等到买武器的人来了，他就开始叫卖。

他先拿起一枝[15]矛，对大家说："你们看，我的长矛是最好的！木柄长长的，矛头又锋利又坚硬，不论[16]多么坚硬的盾它都能刺穿[17]！"然后，他又拿起一面[18]盾，对大家说："再来看看我的盾。我的盾是用最坚固的金属做成的，不论多么锋利的长矛都不能把它刺穿！"

大家看看他的矛，再看看他的盾，觉得都不错。这时有一个买武器的人说："如果我买你的矛，再买你的盾，然后用你的矛去刺你的盾，请问会怎样呢？"

这个卖武器的人一听，不知道怎么回答，只好收起矛和盾回家了。后来，人们把两种互相对立[19]的情况叫做矛盾。如果一个人说话前后不一致，就叫做"自相矛盾"。

自相矛盾 | SIMPLIFIED

很久以前，中國分成[2]了幾個小國，這些小國常常打仗[3]。那時候，人們打仗用的武器[4]是矛和盾。矛是用來進攻[5]的，有長長的木柄[6]，木柄的一頭裝著鋒利[7]的矛頭[8]，又叫長矛。盾是用來防衛[9]的，用堅硬[10]的金屬[11]做成的，打仗時用它擋住[12]身體，可以保護[13]自己不受長矛的攻擊。

一天，有一個人在市場[14]上賣武器。他賣的就是矛和盾。他把矛放在一邊，又把盾放在另外一邊，等到買武器的人來了，他就開始叫賣。

他先拿起一枝[15]矛，對大家說："你們看，我的長矛是最好的！木柄長長的，矛頭又鋒利又堅硬，不論[16]多麼堅硬的盾它都能刺穿[17]！"然後，他又拿起一面[18]盾，對大家說："再來看看我的盾。我的盾是用最堅固的金屬做成的，不論多麼鋒利的長矛都不能把它刺穿！"

大家看看他的矛，再看看他的盾，覺得都不錯。這時有一個買武器的人說："如果我買你的矛，再買你的盾，然後用你的矛去刺你的盾，請問會怎樣呢？"

這個賣武器的人一聽，不知道怎麼回答，只好收起矛和盾回家了。後來，人們把兩種互相對立[19]的情況叫做矛盾。如果一個人說話前後不一致，就叫做"自相矛盾"。

VOCABULARY LIST

	SIMPLIFIED CHARACTERS	TRADITIONAL CHARACTERS	*PINYIN*	PART OF SPEECH	ENGLISH DEFINITION
1.	自	自	zì	n.	self
	相	相	xiāng	adv.	each other
	矛	矛	máo	n.	spear
	盾	盾	dùn	n.	shield
2.	分成	分成	fēnchéng	vc.	to be divided into
3.	打仗	打仗	dǎzhàng	v.	to fight, to be at war
4.	武器	武器	wǔqì	n.	weapon
5.	进攻	進攻	jìngōng	v.	to attack
6.	木柄	木柄	mùbǐng	n.	wooden handle
7.	锋利	鋒利	fēnglì	adj.	sharp
8.	矛头	矛頭	máotóu	n.	the head of a spear
9.	防卫	防衛	fángwèi	v.	to protect oneself
10.	坚硬	堅硬	jiānyìng	adj.	hard, strong
11.	金属	金屬	jīnshǔ	n.	metal
12.	挡住	擋住	dǎngzhù	v.	to block
13.	保护	保護	bǎohù	v.	to protect
14.	市场	市場	shìchǎng	n.	market
15.	枝	枝	zhī	mw.	measure word for a spear

SIMPLIFIED CHARACTERS	TRADITIONAL CHARACTERS	*PINYIN*	PART OF SPEECH	ENGLISH DEFINITION
16. 不论	不論	búlùn	conj.	no matter
17. 刺穿	刺穿	cìchuān	v.	to poke through
18. 面	面	miàn	mw.	measure word for mirrors, flags, etc.
19. 对立	對立	duìlì	v.	to oppose

QUESTIONS

Reading Comprehension

1. At the time this story took place, China was

   A. a strong, unified country.

   B. divided into several small countries.

   C. at war with other countries.

   D. at peace.

2. According to the story, which weapons were used during this period of Chinese history?

   A. Sword and shield

   B. Sword and spear

   C. Spear and shield

   D. Spear and net

3. What is the shield made of?

   A. Wood

   B. Stone

   C. Animal bones

   D. Metal

4. How does the merchant describe his spears?

   A. They are made of the strongest metals.

   B. The tips are long and sharp, and the handles are strong.

   C. They are better than all other spears in China.

   D. The handles are long, and the tips are hard and sharp.

5. What did the customer ask the merchant?

    A.   What will happen if I use your spear to poke through your shield?

    B.   What will happen if I use someone else's spear to poke through your shield?

    C.   What will happen if I use your spear to poke through someone else's shield?

    D.   What will happen if I use my spear to poke through your shield?

6. How did the merchant respond?

    A.   The spear will break.

    B.   The shield will break.

    C.   Both the spear and the shield will break.

    D.   He did not give an answer.

7. This idiom could best be used to describe which of these situations?

    A.   Two friends are fighting about a simple misunderstanding.

    B.   A political candidate promises to cut taxes and increase government spending.

    C.   Two people of equal skill are fighting and neither is able to gain an advantage.

    D.   Many innocent people are dying in a great war.

Discussion

1. If you were the merchant, how would you start selling weapons in the market again? What would you change?

2. Do you know any idioms or proverbs from another culture that similarly explain what a contradiction is?

7

A FROG IN A WELL

井底之蛙 [1]

井底之蛙 [1]

Jǐng dǐ zhī wā

很久以前，在离东海[2]很远的地方有一口井。这口井很小，里面住着一只[3]小青蛙。这只青蛙一直住在这里，它去过的最远的地方就是井台[4]。

每天早上，青蛙在井里找些小虫[5]吃。早饭以后，它跳出来，在井台上晒晒[6]太阳，然后回到井里去休息。吃过午饭以后，它在井里游泳，玩儿。吃完晚饭以后，它坐在井里，看看天上的星星[7]，然后回去睡觉。它的日子就这样一天一天地过去，它觉得自己过得很快乐[8]。

很久以前，在離東海$_2$很遠的地方有一口井。這口井很小，裡面住著一隻$_3$小青蛙。這隻青蛙一直住在這裡，它去過的最遠的地方就是井臺$_4$。

每天早上，青蛙在井里找些小蟲$_5$吃。早飯以後，它跳出來，在井臺上曬曬$_6$太陽，然後回到井里去休息。吃過午飯以後，它在井里游泳，玩兒。吃完晚飯以後，它坐在井里，看看天上的星星$_7$，然後回去睡覺。它的日子就這樣一天一天地過去，它覺得自己過得很快樂$_8$。

有一天，青蛙正在井台上玩儿，路上来了一只大海龟$_9$。它问大海龟："你的家在哪儿？你是从哪儿来的？要上哪儿去？"海龟说："我的家在东海。我从东海来，还要回东海去。"青蛙说："东海是什么地方？你为什么要回那儿去呢？像我这样住在井里多好啊！你看，我每天生活得又快乐又舒服。如果你跟我一起住在这儿，你就再也不想回东海去了。"

　　大海龟听见青蛙把它的井说得那么好，就想下去看看，可是它往井里一看，里面黑黑的，什么也看不见，井口也太小，头和脚都伸$_{10}$不进去，更不用说身体了。

　　大海龟摇摇头$_{11}$，对青蛙说："谢谢你。我不下去了。虽然你的井很舒服，我还是喜欢我的东海。你知道东海有多大吗？它方圆$_{12}$有几千里$_{13}$，我们看不到它的边$_{14}$。你知道东海有多深$_{15}$吗？它有好几里深，海里有很多动物，我们天天在一起玩儿。只有住在那儿，我才觉得真正地快乐！"

　　青蛙听了大海龟的话，才知道井外面还有那么大的世界$_{16}$，觉得自己知道得太少了，而且在一个知道得很多的人面前吹牛$_{17}$，真是可笑。

有一天，青蛙正在井臺上玩兒，路上來了一隻大海龜[9]。它問大海龜："你的家在哪兒？你是從哪兒來的？要上哪兒去？"海龜說："我的家在東海。我從東海來，還要回東海去。"青蛙說："東海是什麼地方？你為什麼要回那兒去呢？像我這樣住在井裡多好啊！你看，我每天生活得又快樂又舒服。如果你跟我一起住在這兒，你就再也不想回東海去了。"

大海龜聽見青蛙把它的井說得那麼好，就想下去看看，可是它往井裡一看，裡面黑黑的，什麼也看不見，井口也太小，頭和腳都伸[10]不進去，更不用說身體了。

大海龜搖搖頭[11]，對青蛙說："謝謝你。我不下去了。雖然你的井很舒服，我還是喜歡我的東海。你知道東海有多大嗎？它方圓[12]有幾千里[13]，我們看不到它的邊[14]。你知道東海有多深[15]嗎？它有好幾裡深，海裡有很多動物，我們天天在一起玩兒。只有住在那兒，我才覺得真正地快樂！"

青蛙聽了大海龜的話，才知道井外面還有那麼大的世界[16]，覺得自己知道得太少了，而且在一個知道得很多的人面前吹牛[17]，真是可笑。

VOCABULARY LIST

SIMPLIFIED CHARACTERS	TRADITIONAL CHARACTERS	*PINYIN*	PART OF SPEECH	ENGLISH DEFINITION
1. 井	井	jǐng	n.	well
底	底	dǐ	n.	bottom
之	之	zhī	part.	indicates possessive
蛙	蛙	wā	n.	frog
2. 东海	東海	dōnghǎi	pn.	the East Sea
3. 只	只	zhī	mw.	measure word for animals
4. 井台	井臺	jǐngtái	n.	the mouth of the well
5. 虫	蟲	chóng	n.	insect, worm
6. 晒	曬	shài	v.	to sunbathe
7. 星	星	xīng	n.	star
8. 快乐	快樂	kuàilè	adj.	happy
9. 海龟	海龜	hǎigūi	n.	sea turtle
10. 伸	伸	shēn	v.	to reach out
11. 摇头	搖頭	yáotóu	v.	to shake one's head
12. 方圆	方圓	fāngyuán	n.	circumference
13. 里	裡	lǐ	n.	a Chinese unit of length (=half kilometer)
14. 边	邊	biān	n.	edge or seashore

A Frog in a Well

	SIMPLIFIED CHARACTERS	TRADITIONAL CHARACTERS	*PINYIN*	PART OF SPEECH	ENGLISH DEFINITION
15.	深	深	shēn	adj.	deep
16.	世界	世界	shìjiè	n.	world
17.	吹牛	吹牛	chuīniú	vo.	to brag

QUESTIONS

Reading Comprehension

1. The frog lives in

   A.   the East Sea.

   B.   a well next to the East Sea.

   C.   a well near the East Sea.

   D.   a well far away from the East Sea.

2. The frog has never been farther than

   A.   the East Sea.

   B.   the mouth of the well.

   C.   the top of the well.

   D.   the temple by the well.

3. The frog begins each morning in the well by

   A.   enjoying the sunshine.

   B.   looking for worms.

   C.   resting in the water.

   D.   swimming in the water.

4. The turtle describes his home as

   A.   large but not deep.

   B.   deep but not large.

   C.   both large and deep.

   D.   neither large nor deep.

5. The turtle thinks that the frog's well is

   A.   an unsuitable place for the frog to live.

   B.   very comfortable, but too deep.

   C.   quieter than the sea.

   D.   comfortable for the frog, but the turtle prefers the sea.

6. After hearing what the turtle said, what is one thing the frog didn't think of?

   A.   It is a big world outside the well.

   B.   The well is quite small.

   C.   The frog is knowledgeable.

   D.   It is foolish to brag.

7. Which sentence best describes the moral of this story?

   A.   The world is not limited to one's own experiences.

   B.   It is better to explore the world than to stay at home.

   C.   People who stay at home will be happier than those who often move.

   D.   Everyone should see the ocean at least once in their life.

Discussion

1. Do you believe that the frog was better off or worse after he met the turtle? Why?

2. Do you know any idioms or proverbs from another culture that have a similar message?

3. Describe a situation in which it would be appropriate to use this idiom.

8

朝三暮四[1]
朝三暮四[1]

Zhāo sān mù sì

从前，有一位老人，住在一座₂大山旁边，山里有很多猴子₃。老人非常喜欢这些猴子，他常常在休息的时候看着它们跳₄来跳去，高高兴兴地玩儿。慢慢地，这些猴子都和老人熟悉₅起来，一点儿也不怕他，还常常跑到他的身边，跟他一起玩儿。就这样，老人和猴子们成了好朋友。

后来，老人在自己家里养了几只猴子。老人和猴子天天在一起，互相都很了解₆。老人对猴子说什么，它们都能听懂₇，他也能看出它们想说什么。

冬天来了，老人给猴子们准备₈了一些果子₉，但是太少了。如果它们每天能少吃几个，还可以吃到第二年春天；如果不省₁₀着点儿，果子就会不够吃。他算₁₁了一下，每只猴子每天只能吃七个果子。

他先给猴子们看了看果子，然后对它们说："果子不够了。从今天起，你们每天每人只能吃七个果子。"猴子们都点头₁₂同意₁₃了。

老人又说："我每天早上给你们三个，晚上给你们四个，好不好？"猴子们一听，都很不高兴，个个摇头不同意，觉得早上只吃三个果子太少了。老人又说："那么早上四个，晚上三个，怎么样？"猴子们一听早上多了一个果子，都很高兴，又叫又跳，一点儿意见₁₄也没有了。

朝三暮四 | SIMPLIFIED

從前，有一位老人，住在一座大山旁邊，山裡有很多猴子[3]。老人非常喜歡這些猴子，他常常在休息的時候看著它們跳[4]來跳去，高高興興地玩兒。慢慢地，這些猴子都和老人熟悉[5]起來，一點兒也不怕他，還常常跑到他的身邊，跟他一起玩兒。就這樣，老人和猴子們成了好朋友。

後來，老人在自己家裡養了幾隻猴子。老人和猴子天天在一起，互相都很了解[6]。老人對猴子說什麼，它們都能聽懂[7]，他也能看出它們想說什麼。

冬天來了，老人給猴子們準備[8]了一些果子[9]，但是太少了。如果它們每天能少吃幾個，還可以吃到第二年春天；如果不省[10]著點兒，果子就會不夠吃。他算[11]了一下，每隻猴子每天只能吃七個果子。

他先給猴子們看了看果子，然後對它們說："果子不夠了。從今天起，你們每天每人只能吃七個果子。"猴子們都點頭[12]同意[13]了。

老人又說："我每天早上給你們三個，晚上給你們四個，好不好？"猴子們一聽，都很不高興，個個搖頭不同意，覺得早上只吃三個果子太少了。老人又說："那麼早上四個，晚上三個，怎麼樣？"猴子們一聽早上多了一個果子，都很高興，又叫又跳，一點兒意見[14]也沒有了。

VOCABULARY LIST

SIMPLIFIED CHARACTERS	TRADITIONAL CHARACTERS	*PINYIN*	PART OF SPEECH	ENGLISH DEFINITION
1. 朝	朝	zhāo	n.	morning
暮	暮	mù	n.	evening
2. 座	座	zuò	mw.	measure word for mountains
3. 猴子	猴子	hóuzi	n.	monkey
4. 跳	跳	tiào	v.	to jump
5. 熟悉	熟悉	shúxī	v.	to get familiar with
6. 了解	了解	liǎojiě	adj.	familiar
7. 懂	懂	dǒng	v.	to understand
8. 准备	準備	zhǔnbèi	v.	to prepare
9. 果子	果子	guǒzi	n.	fruit
10. 省	省	shěng	v.	to save
11. 算	算	suàn	v.	to calculate
12. 点头	點頭	diǎntóu	v.	to nod one's head
13. 同意	同意	tóngyì	v.	to agree
14. 意见	意見	yìjiàn	n.	opinion

Reading Comprehension:

1. Where did the old man live?

   A. At the bottom of a mountain.

   B. In the middle of a mountain.

   C. At the top of a mountain.

   D. Next to a mountain.

2. The old man and the monkeys

   A. are not familiar with each other.

   B. know each other very well.

   C. depend on each other for food.

   D. are afraid of each other.

3. How many fruits did the old man offer each monkey each day?

   A. Three

   B. Four

   C. Seven

   D. Eight

4. At first, the old man offered each monkey

   A. three fruits in the morning and four fruits in the evening.

   B. four fruits in the morning and three fruits in the evening.

   C. four fruits in the morning and four fruits in the evening.

   D. eight fruits in the morning and none in the evening.

5. What were the monkeys' reaction to this offer?

    A.   Most of them agreed.

    B.   The head monkey disagreed.

    C.   Most of them disagreed.

    D.   None of them agreed.

6. The monkeys finally agreed to eat

    A.   three fruits in the morning and four fruits in the evening.

    B.   four fruits in the morning and three fruits in the evening.

    C.   four fruits in the morning and four fruits in the evening.

    D.   eight fruits in the morning and none in the evening.

7. Which sentence best describes the moral of this story?

    A.   Early gains don't always lead to overall success.

    B.   The big picture is more important than the details.

    C.   It is better to wait patiently than to act rashly.

    D.   The presentation of an idea can be more important than the idea itself.

Discussion

1. In your opinion, did the old man take advantage of the monkeys? Did the monkeys benefit in any way?

2. Do you know any idioms or proverbs from another culture that have a similar message?

3. Describe a situation in which it would be appropriate to use this idiom.

9

CARVING A MARK ON A BOAT TO
LOOK FOR A LOST SWORD

刻 舟 求 剑 ₁
刻 舟 求 劍 ₁

Kè zhōu qiú jiàn

从前，有一个人坐船$_2$去办事，他身上带着一把宝$_3$剑。当船到了江心$_4$的时候，他的剑不小心掉$_5$到江里去了。船上的人都为他着急，觉得这太可惜$_6$了，叫他赶快$_7$跳到水里去捞$_8$。

可是这个人却一点儿也不着急。他拿出一把小刀$_9$，在自己的座位旁边刻了一个记号$_{10}$，然后对大家说："没关系，我在这儿刻上记号了。等船到了对岸$_{11}$，我只要从这个有记号的地方跳下去，就可以找到我的剑了。"

船到了岸以后，这个人就从那个有记号的地方跳到江里，去捞他的宝剑，可是什么也没有捞到。

有一个老人对他说："年轻人$_{12}$！虽然你的宝剑掉下去的时候你是坐在这个座位上，可是那时船在江心，你的宝剑掉在江心了！现在船已经到了岸，离江心那么远，你再从这个地方跳下去，怎么能找到你的宝剑呢？"这个人听了，才知道自己做错了。

刻舟求剑 | SIMPLIFIED

從前，有一個人坐船[2]去辦事，他身上帶著一把寶劍[3]。當船到了江心[4]的時候，他的劍不小心掉[5]到江裡去了。船上的人都為他著急，覺得這太可惜[6]了，叫他趕快[7]跳到水裡去撈[8]。

可是這個人卻一點兒也不著急。他拿出一把小刀[9]，在自己的座位旁邊刻了一個記號[10]，然後對大家說："沒關係，我在這兒刻上記號了。等船到了對岸[11]，我只要從這個有記號的地方跳下去，就可以找到我的劍了。"

船到了岸以後，這個人就從那個有記號的地方跳到江裡，去撈他的寶劍，可是什麼也沒有撈到。

有一個老人對他說："年輕人[12]！雖然你的寶劍掉下去的時候你是坐在這個座位上，可是那時船在江心，你的寶劍掉在江心了！現在船已經到了岸，離江心那麼遠，你再從這個地方跳下去，怎麼能找到你的寶劍呢？"這個人聽了，才知道自己做錯了。

VOCABULARY LIST

	SIMPLIFIED CHARACTERS	TRADITIONAL CHARACTERS	*PINYIN*	PART OF SPEECH	ENGLISH DEFINITION
1.	刻	刻	kè	v.	to carve
	舟	舟	zhōu	n.	boat
	求	求	qiú	v.	to look for
	剑	劍	jiàn	n.	sword
2.	船	船	chuán	n.	boat
3.	宝	寶	bǎo	adj.	valuable
4.	江心	江心	jiāngxīn	n.	middle of the river
5.	掉	掉	diào	v.	to drop, to fall
6.	可惜	可惜	kěxī	adj.	pitiful
7.	赶快	趕快	gǎnkuài	adv.	quickly
8.	捞	撈	lāo	v.	to retrieve
9.	刀	刀	dāo	n.	knife, dagger
10.	记号	記號	jìhào	n.	mark
11.	对岸	對岸	duì'àn	n.	the opposite shore
12.	年轻人	年輕	niánqīngrén	n.	young man

QUESTIONS

1. Where did the young man drop his sword?

   A. Near the river bank.

   B. On the shore.

   C. Near the ocean.

   D. In the middle of the river.

2. How did the young man feel when he dropped his sword?

   A. He felt worried.

   B. He did not feel worried.

   C. He thought it was a shame.

   D. He felt unhappy.

3. Where did the young man carve a mark?

   A. Next to his seat.

   B. The middle of the boat.

   C. The bow of the boat.

   D. The stern of the boat.

4. Why did the young man carve a mark on the boat?

   A. Because he was angry.

   B. To check the level of the water.

   C. So he could find his sword later.

   D. To see if the knife was as sharp as his sword.

5. What did the young man do when the ship landed ashore?

   A.   He jumped into the river and found his sword.

   B.   He jumped into the river but failed to find his sword.

   C.   He swam to the middle of the river and found his sword.

   D.   He swam to the middle of the river but failed to find his sword.

6. Which sentence best describes the moral of this story?

   A.   Precious items are not the most important treasure.

   B.   Adhering to inflexible notions will cause problems when the situation changes.

   C.   It is better to travel by land than by water.

   D.   Ignoring the advice of others will leave you isolated.

7. Which of these reasons best explains why a parent or teacher might tell this story to a child?

   A.   To emphasize the importance of hard work.

   B.   To emphasize the importance of keeping a careful eye on his/her possessions.

   C.   To encourage the child to think outside the box.

   D.   To emphasize the importance of considering a situation before acting.

Discussion

1. Do you know any idioms or proverbs from another culture that have a similar message?

2. Describe a situation in which it would be appropriate to use this idiom.

10

AN OLD MAN ON THE FRONTIER LOSES HIS HORSE

塞 翁 失 马 ₁

塞 翁 失 馬 ₁

Sài wēng shī mǎ

从前，有一个老人和他的儿子住在边境₂上，人们都叫他"塞翁₃"。塞翁跟村子里的人一样，养了很多马。每天早上，他和儿子都把马带到很远的地方去吃草₄，晚上再把它们带回家来。

有一天，塞翁的一匹₅马不见了。他找啊找啊，找了好几天，可是找不到。村里的人知道了，都觉得很可惜，大家都来安慰₆他。可是他们到他家的时候，看到他一点也不伤心₇。大家问他为什么不伤心。他说："马丢₈了，我当然₉不高兴。不过丢了就丢了吧，我觉得不要太伤心，谁知道以后会怎么样呢？"

几个月过去了，塞翁丢的那匹马自己回来了，而且还带回来几匹高大漂亮的野马₁₀。村里的人为他高

從前，有一個老人和他的兒子住在邊境[2]上，人們都叫他"塞翁[3]"。塞翁跟村子裡的人一樣，養了很多馬。每天早上，他和兒子都把馬帶到很遠的地方去吃草[4]，晚上再把它們帶回家來。

有一天，塞翁的一匹[5]馬不見了。他找啊找啊，找了好幾天，可是找不到。村裡的人知道了，都覺得很可惜，大家都來安慰[6]他。可是他們到他家的時候，看到他一點也不傷心[7]。大家問他為什麼不傷心。他說："馬丟[8]了，我當然[9]不高興。不過丟了就丟了吧，我覺得不要太傷心，誰知道以後會怎麼樣呢？"

幾個月過去了，塞翁丟的那匹馬自己回來了，而且還帶回來幾匹高大漂亮的野馬[10]。村裡的人為他高兴，都到他家来庆祝。可是他们到他家的时候，却看到他并不特别₁₁高兴。大家问他为什么，他说："马回来了，而且还带回几匹野马，我当然高兴。可是野马不驯服₁₂就卖不出去，要驯服它们又很不容易。谁知道它们会不会给我家带来什么坏₁₃事呢？"

塞翁说得很对，这些野马真的很不容易驯服，驯服它们的时候，塞翁的儿子从马背₁₄上掉下来，受伤₁₅了，成了一个残疾₁₆人。村子里的人听说塞翁的儿子受伤了，都来安慰他。可是塞翁并不特别伤心，他对大家说："我的儿子虽然受伤了，成了残疾人，但是谁知道这不是一件好事呢？"

不久，边境上发生了战争₁₇，健康的₁₈男人都要去打仗。塞翁的儿子因为是个残疾人，不能去，只好留在家里。打仗的时候，很多健康的男人都死了，而塞翁的儿子却因为是个残疾人，活₁₉下来了。

興，都到他家來慶祝。可是他們到他家的時候，卻看到他並不特別[11]高興。大家問他為什麼，他說："馬回來了，而且還帶回幾匹野馬，我當然高興。可是野馬不馴服[12]就賣不出去，要馴服它們又很不容易。誰知道它們會不會給我家帶來什麼壞[13]事呢？"

塞翁說得很對，這些野馬真的很不容易馴服，馴服它們的時候，塞翁的兒子從馬背[14]上掉下來，受傷[15]了，成了一個殘疾[16]人。村子裡的人聽說塞翁的兒子受傷了，都來安慰他。可是塞翁並不特別傷心，他對大家說："我的兒子雖然受傷了，成了殘疾人，但是誰知道這不是一件好事呢？"

不久，邊境上發生了戰爭[17]，健康的[18]男人都要去打仗。塞翁的兒子因為是個殘疾人，不能去，只好留在家裡。打仗的時候，很多健康的男人都死了，而塞翁的兒子卻因為是個殘疾人，活[19]下來了。

VOCABULARY LIST

	SIMPLIFIED CHARACTERS	TRADITIONAL CHARACTERS	*PINYIN*	PART OF SPEECH	ENGLISH DEFINITION
1.	塞	塞	sài	n.	border, frontier
	翁	翁	wēng	n.	elderly man
	失	失	shī	v.	to lose
	马	馬	mǎ	n.	horse
2.	边境	邊境	biānjìng	n.	border
3.	塞翁	塞翁	Sàiwēng	pn.	name of a person
4.	草	草	cǎo	n.	grass
5.	匹	匹	pǐ	mw.	measure word for horses
6.	安慰	安慰	ānwèi	v.	to comfort
7.	伤心	傷心	shāngxīn	adj.	heartbroken
8.	丢	丢	diū	v.	to lose
9.	当然	當然	dāngrán	adv.	surely
10.	野马	野馬	yěmǎ	n.	wild horse
11.	特别	特別	tèbié	adv.	specially
12.	驯服	馴服	xùnfú	v.	to tame
13.	坏	壞	huài	adj.	bad
14.	马背	馬背	mǎbèi	n.	horseback

SIMPLIFIED CHARACTERS	TRADITIONAL CHARACTERS	*PINYIN*	PART OF SPEECH	ENGLISH DEFINITION
15. 受伤	受傷	shòu shāng	vo.	to be injured
16. 残疾	殘疾	cánjí	n.	disability
17. 战争	戰爭	zhànzhēng	n.	war
18. 健康的	健康的	jiànkāngde	adj.	healthy
19. 活	活	huó	v.	to be alive

An Old Man on the Frontier Loses His Horse

QUESTIONS

1. After he loses his horse, how does the old man say he feels?

    A. Heartbroken

    B. Happy

    C. Confused

    D. Not happy

2. What happened when the old man's horse returned?

    A. The horse brought back some wild horses.

    B. The horse kicked the old man's son.

    C. The horse was disabled.

    D. The horse was sick.

3. After the old man's horse returned, how did the villagers expect him to feel?

    A. Heartbroken

    B. Happy

    C. Confused

    D. Not happy

4. Why was the old man not particularly happy when his horse returned?

    A. The horse was sick.

    B. His son was kicked by the horse.

    C. The wild horses are hard to tame.

    D. The horse would leave soon.

5. Why did the old man's son not have to go to war?

    A.   He was killed after falling off a horse.

    B.   He rode away on a wild horse.

    C.   He was transformed into a horse.

    D.   He was disabled after falling off a horse.

6. What happened during the war?

    A.   The old man died.

    B.   The old man's son died.

    C.   The old man's horse died.

    D.   Many strong and healthy men died.

7. Which sentence best describes the moral of this story?

    A.   Things always work out for the best in the end.

    B.   No one can predict the future, so there is no point in trying.

    C.   Bad situations may turn out well and good situations may turn out poorly.

    D.   Take advantage of each opportunity when it appears.

Discussion

1. Do you know any idioms or proverbs from another culture that have a similar message?

2. Describe a situation in which it would be appropriate to use this idiom.

II

SAYINGS OF IMPORTANT HISTORICAL FIGURES

第二章 名人轶事
第二章 名人轶事

11

ONE OUT OF EVERY THREE MUST BE MY MENTOR

三 人 行 必 有 我 师
三 人 行 必 有 我 師

Sān rén xíng bì yǒu wǒ shī

Confucius (551–479 B.C.E.) laid the foundation of traditional Chinese culture and is one of the most influential philosophers in world history. He taught the principles of maintaining social order and familial harmony, upholding morals and rituals, revering learning and education, and being a benevolent, righteous, and modest person.

孔子[1]是中国有名[2]的思想家[3]，他一共教过三千多个学生。他常常说："三人行[4]，必有我师。"他觉得每三个人中，就有一个人可以做他的老师，因为每个人都有长处[5]让他学习。

有一天，孔子和他的学生见到了一个国王[6]。国王说："孔子，你是有名的大师，你能用线[7]穿过[8]这个珠子[9]吗？"

孔子把珠子拿过来看了看，看见珠子中间有一个小孔[10]，小孔又小又弯弯曲曲[11]。他和他的学生想了很多办法，都没把线穿过去。

这时候，有一个小女孩从旁边走过。她看见孔子穿不过去，就对他说："这很容易。你把线拴[12]在一只蚂蚁[13]上，让蚂蚁从珠子的孔里爬[14]过去，线就能穿过去了。"

孔子听了，赶快找了一只蚂蚁，很快就把线穿过去了。

这件事让孔子想了很久。他对学生说："你看，一个小女孩子也可以教我们，当我们的老师。我们真应该好好向每个人学习啊。"

孔子₁是中國有名₂的思想家₃，他一共教過三千多個學生。他常常說："三人行₄，必有我師。"他覺得每三個人中，就有一個人可以做他的老師，因為每個人都有長處₅讓他學習。

　　有一天，孔子和他的學生見到了一個國王₆。國王說："孔子，你是有名的大師，你能用線₇穿過₈這個珠子₉嗎？"

　　孔子把珠子拿過來看了看，看見珠子中間有一個小孔₁₀，小孔又小又彎彎曲曲₁₁。他和他的學生想了很多辦法，都沒把線穿過去。

　　這時候，有一個小女孩從旁邊走過。她看見孔子穿不過去，就對他說："這很容易。你把線拴₁₂在一隻螞蟻₁₃上，讓螞蟻從珠子的孔裡爬₁₄過去，線就能穿過去了。"

　　孔子聽了，趕快找了一隻螞蟻，很快就把線穿過去了。

　　這件事讓孔子想了很久。他對學生說："你看，一個小女孩子也可以教我們，當我們的老師。我們真應該好好向每個人學習啊。"

VOCABULARY LIST

SIMPLIFIED CHARACTERS	TRADITIONAL CHARACTERS	*PINYIN*	PART OF SPEECH	ENGLISH DEFINITION
1. 孔子	孔子	Kǒngzǐ	pn.	Confucius
2. 有名	有名	yǒumíng	adj.	famous
3. 思想家	思想家	sīxiǎngjiā	n.	philosopher, thinker
4. 行	行	xíng	v.	to walk
5. 长处	長處	chángchù	n.	strong points
6. 国王	國王	guówáng	n.	king
7. 线	線	xiàn	n.	thread
8. 穿过	穿過	chuānguo	vc.	to pass through
9. 珠子	珠子	zhūzi	n.	beads
10. 小孔	小孔	xiǎokǒng	n.	small holes
11. 弯弯曲曲	彎彎曲曲	wānwānqūqū	adj.	crooked
12. 拴	拴	shuān	v.	to tie
13. 蚂蚁	螞蟻	mǎyǐ	n.	ant
14. 爬	爬	pá	v.	to crawl

QUESTIONS

Reading Comprehension

1. In the beginnng of the story, Confucius is described as a famous

    A. educator.

    B. philosopher.

    C. politician.

    D. economist.

2. According to the story, how many people did Confucius teach?

    A. Less than 3,000

    B. Over 3,000

    C. Exactly 3,000

    D. Over 30,000

3. What did the king ask Confucius to do?

    A. Make an ant go through a small bead.

    B. Thread a string through a bead without using a needle.

    C. Thread a string through a small bead.

    D. Find a young girl who was wiser than Confucius.

4. Why is the task so difficult?

    A. The bead does not have a hole in it.

    B. The hole of the bead is crooked.

    C. It is hard for Confucius to work together with his students.

    D. There is a time limit set by the king.

5. Who came up with the solution eventually?

   A. Confucius

   B. Confucius' student

   C. The king

   D. A little girl

6. What is the main idea of this story?

   A. Confucius was a famous philosopher in China.

   B. You can thread a bead by tying string to an ant.

   C. You can learn something from everyone.

   D. Confucius was not as wise as people think.

7. Which reason best explains why a parent or teacher would tell this story to a child?

   A. To teach the child about Confucius' life and philosophy.

   B. To explain how to accomplish a difficult task.

   C. To explain the importance of listening to authority figures like parents and teachers.

   D. To teach the child to be open-minded and not condescending toward others.

Discussion

1. Have you heard of Confucius before? What have you heard about him or his philosophy?

2. Are there any Western philosophers who expressed ideas similar to those Confucius did in this story? Are there any philosophers who expressed opposing views? Who were they, and what were their ideas?

12

孟母三迁
孟母三遷

Mèngmǔ sān qiān

Mencius (372–289 B.C.E.) was one of Confucius' students and a famous philosopher. Following Confucius' philosophical and educational theories, he also emphasized learning, education, and rituals to cultivate qualities such as modesty, filial piety, and fraternal love. He believed that humans are born good-natured but are corrupted by the negative influences of society.

孟 子₁是孔子的学生，也是很有名的思想家。
孟子小的时候，他家里很穷₂。他的父
亲死得很早，母亲抚养₃他。孟子小时候不喜欢
学习，只想玩儿，他的母亲想了很多办法来帮助
他。开始他们住在一个墓地₄旁边，小孟子和别的
孩子一起，学着大人哭，玩死人的事儿。孟子妈
妈看了很生气，她说："这不行，我不能让我的孩
子玩这个，我们不能住在这里。"

孟子和他妈妈搬家了。他们搬到一个集市旁
边。孟子又和别的孩子一起，学着大人买卖东
西。孟子的妈妈又说："不行，这里也不行，不适
合₅我的孩子住。"

他们又搬家了。这一次他们搬到了一个学校旁
边。小孟子和别的孩子一起，跟着老师学习，慢慢
儿喜欢念书了。孟子的妈妈看了很高兴，
说:"这才是适合我儿子住的地方。"

因为孟子的母亲非常注意₆让孟子从
小就接受₇好的教育₈，所以孟子长大以后
成了有名的思想家。

这就是"孟母三迁"₉的故事。后来人
们就用这个故事来说明₁₀只有接近₁₁好的环
境₁₂，才能养成好的习惯，成为有用的人。

孟 子[1]是孔子的學生，也是很有名的思想家。

孟子小的時候，他家裡很窮[2]。他的父親死得很早，母親撫養[3]他。孟子小時候不喜歡學習，只想玩兒，他的母親想了很多辦法來幫助他。開始他們住在一個墓地[4]旁邊，小孟子和別的孩子一起，學著大人哭，玩死人的事兒。孟子媽媽看了很生氣，她說："這不行，我不能讓我的孩子玩這個，我們不能住在這裡。"

孟子和他媽媽搬家了。他們搬到一個集市旁邊。孟子又和別的孩子一起，學著大人買賣東西。孟子的媽媽又說："不行，這裡也不行，不適合[5]我的孩子住。"

他們又搬家了。這一次他們搬到了一個學校旁邊。小孟子和別的孩子一起，跟著老師學習，慢慢兒喜歡唸書了。孟子的媽媽看了很高興，說："這才是適合我兒子住的地方。"

因為孟子的母親非常注意[6]讓孟子從小就接受[7]好的教育[8]，所以孟子長大以後成了有名的思想家。

這就是"孟母三遷"[9]的故事。後來人們就用這個故事來說明[10]只有接近[11]好的環境[12]，才能養成好的習慣，成為有用的人。

VOCABULARY LIST

	SIMPLIFIED CHARACTERS	TRADITIONAL CHARACTERS	*PINYIN*	PART OF SPEECH	ENGLISH DEFINITION
1.	孟子	孟子	Mèngzǐ	pn.	Mencius
2.	穷	窮	qióng	adj.	poor
3.	抚养	撫養	fúyǎng	v.	to raise
4.	墓地	墓地	mùdì	adj.	cemetery
5.	适合	適合	shìhé	adj.	suitable
6.	注意	注意	zhùyì	v.	to pay attention to
7.	接受	接受	jiēshòu	v.	to receive
8.	教育	教育	jiàoyù	v./n.	to educate, education
9.	孟母三迁	孟母三遷	Mèngmǔ sān qiān	n.	Mencius' mother moved three times
10.	说明	說明	shūomíng	v.	to show
11.	接近	接近	jiējìn	v.	to be around
12.	环境	環境	huánjìng	n.	environment

QUESTIONS

1. Mencius is

   A. Confucius' teacher.

   B. the teacher of Confucius' teacher.

   C. Confucius' student.

   D. the student of Confucius' student.

2. Why does Mencius' mother raise him by herself?

   A. Mencius' parents were divorced.

   B. Mencius' father died early.

   C. Mencius loves studying with his mother.

   D. Mencius loves playing with his mother.

3. Mencius and his mother first lived by a

   A. school.

   B. market.

   C. graveyard.

   D. temple.

4. Where did Mencius and his mother move to first?

   A. Along a river

   B. Near a mountain

   C. By a school

   D. Next to a market

5. Mencius' mother thought the most suitable house was the one by the

   A. school.

   B. market.

   C. graveyard.

   D. temple.

6. What led to Mencius' success?

   A. A spacious living environment.

   B. Good teachers and classmates.

   C. Intelligence and hard work.

   D. Receiving high-quality education since childhood.

7. What is the main idea of this story?

   A. Environment is important to a person's development.

   B. A mother's love knows no bounds.

   C. Having a difficult childhood can make a person stronger.

   D. Mencius was a student of Confucius and a famous Chinese philosopher.

Discussion

1. How does Mencius' mother feel about her son learning to buy and sell goods? What does this imply about the traditional Chinese view toward merchants and commerce?

2. What values do parents in your culture place the most importance on regarding their children's education? How is this similar to or different from the values that Mencius' mother thought were important?

3. Online, research Mencius and his philosophy. What are some of the core ideas of his philosophy? Are any of these ideas reflected in modern society, either in China or in your own culture?

13

KONG RONG OFFERS THE BEST PEARS
TO HIS BROTHERS

孔 融 让 梨
孔 融 讓 梨

Kǒng Róng ràng lí

Kong Rong (153–208 C.E.) was a descendant of Confucius who lived during
the Three Kingdoms period. His essays and poems were highly praised by
both contemporaries and later literati. He also enjoyed a good reputation for
practicing proper manners and maintaining familial harmony as a true follower
of Confucius.

孔融₁是孔子的第二十代₂子孙₃，他跟孔子一样也是中国有名的思想家。孔融从小就是个好孩子。

孔融出生在一个大家庭里。他有五个哥哥，一个弟弟。孔融四岁的时候，有一天，爸爸给孩子们吃梨₄，他让孔融先拿。孔融看了看盘子里的梨，伸出手去，拿了一个最小最不好的。

爸爸看了，觉得很奇怪，就问孔融："这么多的梨，我让你先拿，你为什么只拿了一个最小的呢？"

孔融笑着说："我年纪₅小，应该吃小的；大的留给哥哥们吃吧。"

爸爸又问："那弟弟呢，他的年纪不是更小吗？"

孔融又说："我比弟弟大，所以应该把大的梨留给弟弟吃。"

爸爸听了，很高兴，说："孔融真是一个好孩子。"

大家都夸₆孔融是个有爱心的好孩子，说他真是孔子的好子孙。

孔融让梨 | SIMPLIFIED

孔融₁是孔子的第二十代₂子孫₃，他跟孔子一樣也是中國有名的思想家。孔融從小就是個好孩子。

孔融出生在一個大家庭裡。他有五個哥哥，一個弟弟。孔融四歲的時候，有一天，爸爸給孩子們吃梨₄，他讓孔融先拿。孔融看了看盤子裡的梨，伸出手去，拿了一個最小最不好的。

爸爸看了，覺得很奇怪，就問孔融："這麼多的梨，我讓你先拿，你為什麼只拿了一個最小的呢？"

孔融笑著說："我年紀₅小，應該吃小的；大的留給哥哥們吃吧。"

爸爸又問："那弟弟呢，他的年紀不是更小嗎？"

孔融又說："我比弟弟大，所以應該把大的梨留給弟弟吃。"

爸爸聽了，很高興，說："孔融真是一個好孩子。"

大家都誇₆孔融是個有愛心的好孩子，說他真是孔子的好子孫。

VOCABULARY LIST

SIMPLIFIED CHARACTERS	TRADI-TIONAL CHARACTERS	*PINYIN*	PART OF SPEECH	ENGLISH DEFINITION
1. 孔融	孔融	Kǒng Róng	pn.	Kong Rong, a descendant of Confucius
2. 代	代	dài	n.	generation
3. 子孙	子孫	zǐsūn	n.	descendant
4. 梨	梨	lí	n.	pear
5. 年纪	年紀	niánji	n.	age
6. 夸	誇	kuā	v.	to praise

QUESTIONS

Reading Comprehension

1. What information can we infer from the beginning of the story?

   A. The political status of Kong Rong.

   B. The achievement of Kong Rong.

   C. The relationship between Kong Rong and Confucius.

   D. The relationship between Kong Rong and Mencius.

2. How many brothers did Kong Rong have?

   A. One

   B. Five

   C. Six

   D. Seven

3. How old was Kong Rong at the time of this story?

   A. Three

   B. Four

   C. Five

   D. Six

4. What did Kong Rong do?

   A. He chose the smallest pear.

   B. He chose the second smallest pear.

   C. He was the second-to-last one to choose a pear.

   D. He was the last one to choose a pear.

5. What was his reason for doing so?

   A. His selfishness

   B. His age compared to his brothers

   C. His eating habits

   D. His high level of education

6. What is the main idea of this story?

   A. Kong Rong was a descendant of Confucius.

   B. The eldest sibling should be responsible for the younger siblings.

   C. Kong Rong was the most intelligent of his brothers.

   D. Kong Rong was selfless in giving his brothers the best pears.

7. Which reason best explains why a parent or teacher might tell this story to a child?

   A. To teach the child the importance of honoring one's parents.

   B. To teach the child to study hard and become a successful adult.

   C. To show the eldest child how to take care of his/her younger siblings.

   D. To show the child how he/she should treat his/her siblings.

Discussion

1. Is there a proverb or story from your culture that shows how siblings should treat each other?

2. Online, research Kong Rong. What is the period of Chinese history that Kong Rong lived during called? What famous Chinese novel was later written about this period?

14

GRINDING DOWN AN IRON PESTLE TO A NEEDLE

铁 杵 磨 成 针[1]

鐵 杵 磨 成 針[1]

Tiě chǔ mó chéng zhēn

Li Bai (701–762 C.E.) was a Chinese poet who lived during the Tang Dynasty (618–907 C.E.). He is sometimes called Li Bo or Li Po. Called the "Poet Immortal," Li Bai is often regarded as one of the greatest poets in China's history. Approximately 1,100 of his poems remain today.

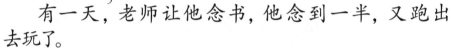

大诗人[2]李白写了很多优美[3]的诗[4]。直到今天，人们还是很喜欢读他的诗，说他的故事。"铁杵磨成针"是他小时候的故事。

李白小的时候一点也不喜欢念书，常常逃学[5]，到学校外面去玩。

有一天[5]，老师让他念书，他念到一半，又跑出去玩了。

这天很热，小李白就跑到河边去玩。他看见一位老奶奶[6]拿着一根大铁杵在一块大石头[7]上磨呀磨呀。老奶奶磨得很认真[8]，满头都是汗[9]。

小李白觉得很奇怪，就问："你在做什么呀，老奶奶？"

老奶奶一边磨着，一边说："我在磨这根铁杵呀。"

小李白觉得更奇怪了，又问："磨这个做什么啊？"

老奶奶抬起头，看了看李白说，"做一根针呀。"

"什么？！"小李白大叫[10]起来，"你想把这么粗的铁杵磨成小小的针？！这可是要多少年的时间呀！"

"你说得很对，这是要很长的时间。可是，只要我一直磨下去，我一定能把它磨成针的。"

老人的话深深地[11]打动[12]了小李白，从此，他认真学习，成了一位大诗人。

后来，人们常常把"铁杵磨成针"用来说明一个人只要有认真，就一定能够成功[13]，做到他想要做的事情。

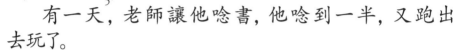

大詩人[2]李白寫了很多優美[3]的詩[4]。直到今天，人們還是很喜歡讀他的詩，說他的故事。"鐵杵磨成針"是他小時候的故事。

李白小的時候一點也不喜歡唸書，常常逃學[5]，到學校外面去玩。

有一天，老師讓他唸書，他唸到一半，又跑出去玩了。

這天很熱，小李白就跑到河邊去玩。他看見一位老奶奶[6]拿著一根大鐵杵在一塊大石頭[7]上磨呀磨呀。老奶奶磨得很認真[8]，滿頭都是汗[9]。

小李白覺得很奇怪，就問："你在做什麼呀，老奶奶？"

老奶奶一邊磨著，一邊說："我在磨這根鐵杵呀。"

小李白覺得更奇怪了，又問："磨這個做什麼啊？"

老奶奶抬起頭，看了看李白說，"做一根針呀。"

"什麼？！"小李白大叫[10]起來，"你想把這麼粗的鐵杵磨成小小的針？！這可是要多少年的時間呀！"

"你說得很對，這是要很長的時間。可是，只要我一直磨下去，我一定能把它磨成針的。"

老人的話深深地[11]打動[12]了小李白，從此，他認真學習，成了一位大詩人。

後來，人們常常把"鐵杵磨成針"用來說明一個人只要有認真，就一定能夠成功[13]，做到他想要做的事情。

VOCABULARY LIST

SIMPLIFIED CHARACTERS	TRADITIONAL CHARACTERS	*PINYIN*	PART OF SPEECH	ENGLISH DEFINITION
1. 铁杆	鐵杆	tiě chǔ	n.	iron pestle
磨	磨	mó	v.	to grind
针	針	zhēn	n.	needle
2. 诗人	詩人	shīrén	n.	poet
3. 优美	優美	yōuměi	adj.	beautiful, elegant
4. 诗	詩	shī	n.	poem
5. 逃学	逃學	táoxué	vo.	to play truant
6. 老奶奶	老奶奶	lǎo nǎinai	n.	grandmother, elderly woman
7. 石头	石頭	shítou	n.	stone
8. 认真	認真	rènzhēn	adv.	seriously, diligently
9. 汗	汗	hàn	n.	sweat
10. 大叫	大叫	dàjiào	v.	to yell
11. 深深地	深深地	shēnshen de	adv.	deeply
12. 打动	打動	dǎdòng	vc.	to be moved
13. 成功	成功	chénggōng	v.	to succeed

Grinding Down an Iron Pestle to a Needle

QUESTIONS

Reading Comprehension

1. Li Bai was a

   A. poet.

   B. philosopher.

   C. teacher.

   D. composer.

2. What did Li Bai like to do when he was young?

   A. Write poems

   B. Read books

   C. Attend classes

   D. Skip school

3. When his teacher told him to read, Li Bai

   A. read the entire book and then went out to play.

   B. went right out to play.

   C. read half the book and then went out to play.

   D. started to grind down an iron pestle.

4. Where was the old woman when Li Bai found her?

   A. On a boat

   B. Beside the river

   C. Under a tree

   D. On a pile of rocks

5. How long would it take to make a needle out of an iron pestle?

    A. A couple of weeks

    B. A couple of months

    C. Many years

    D. An entire lifetime

6. After talking to the old woman, Li Bai was

    A. shocked.

    B. moved.

    C. discouraged.

    D. provoked.

7. The phrase "Grinding Down an Iron Pestle to Make a Needle" is analogous to

    A. parents working hard to ensure their children receive a good education.

    B. an old woman having difficulty with an exhausting physical task.

    C. a person grinding their teeth in frustration.

    D. a student studying hard to become a successful adult.

Discussion

1. Do you think this story really happened? Why or why not?

2. Is there a proverb or story in your own culture that uses a famous person to teach a similar lesson?

3. Online, research Li Bai and his work and answer these questions. When did Li Bai live? Where there any major events during his lifetime? What themes are common in his work? Then, choose one of his writings and present it your class in Chinese or an English translation.

15

BRINGING A BIRCH AND BEGGING FOR A FLOGGING

负 荆 请 罪 ₁

負 荊 請 罪 ₁

Fù jīng qǐng zuì

Lian Po, a general, and Lin Xiangru, a statesman, were both prominent officials of the State of Zhao during the Warring States period (475–221 B.C.E.) when China was broken up into several small states. Zhao was an enemy of the State of Qin, which eventually succeeded in uniting China.

廉颇₂是赵国₃的大将军₄。他打过很多胜仗₅，立₆过很多功劳₇。赵国的国王很喜欢他，所以廉颇很骄傲₈。后来，一位叫蔺相如₉的人也帮赵国作了很多大事，立了很多功劳，赵王也很喜欢他，让他作了官₁₀，官比廉颇将军还大。

廉颇很不高兴，他说："我是赵国的大将军，打了很多胜仗，立了很多功劳。蔺相如的官还比我的大。哼！我要是见到蔺相如，就要对他不客气！"

廉颇的话蔺相如听到了，他就很小心，到处躲₁₁着廉颇。

有一天，蔺相如看见廉颇来了，就到旁边去躲一躲，让廉颇先走。

蔺相如的仆人很生气，他们都说蔺相如不应该这么怕廉颇。

蔺相如听了，笑着问他们："你们看廉颇将军和秦国₁₂的国王，哪一个更可怕₁₃？"

仆人们说："那当然是秦国的国王更可怕了。"

蔺相如说："对呀！秦国的国王那么可怕，人人都怕他，可是我不怕。那为什么我怕廉颇将军呢？

廉頗₂是趙國₃的大將軍₄。他打過很多勝仗₅，立₆過很多功勞₇。趙國的國王很喜歡他，所以廉頗很驕傲₈。後來，一位叫藺相如₉的人也幫趙國作了很多大事，立了很多功勞，趙王也很喜歡他，讓他作了官₁₀，官比廉頗將軍還大。

廉頗很不高興，他說："我是趙國的大將軍，打了很多勝仗，立了很多功勞。藺相如的官還比我的大。哼！我要是見到藺相如，就要對他不客氣！"

廉頗的話藺相如聽到了，他就很小心，到處躲₁₁著廉頗。

有一天，藺相如看見廉頗來了，就到旁邊去躲一躲，讓廉頗先走。

藺相如的僕人很生氣，他們都說藺相如不應該這麼怕廉頗。

藺相如聽了，笑著問他們："你們看廉頗將軍和秦國₁₂的國王，哪一個更可怕₁₃？"

僕人們說："那當然是秦國的國王更可怕了。"

藺相如說："對呀！秦國的國王那麼可怕，人人都怕他，可是我不怕。那為什麼我怕廉頗將軍呢？因為秦國不因为秦国不来进攻赵国，就是因为有我和廉颇将军。要是我们两个人不和[14]，秦国就会来进攻。我躲着廉颇将军，不是怕他，而是为了我们的国家啊。"

后来，有人告诉了廉颇这些话。廉颇听了以后，想了很久，知道自己错了。他就背着一根很粗的荆条，到蔺相如家里去请罪。廉颇见了蔺相如就说："我错了，我太骄傲了。您为了国家，对我这么好。请您用这根荆条打我吧。"

蔺相如赶快把荆条从廉颇背上拿下来，说："廉颇将军不要这样。我们两个人都是赵国的大将军，应该一起为国家服务。您能够理解[15]我，我已经很高兴了，怎么还能让您来给我道歉[16]呢。"

就这样，他们成了最好的朋友，一起为赵国立了很多功劳。

"负荆请罪"就是说，知道自己错了，就去向别人道歉。

來進攻趙國，就是因為有我和廉頗將軍。要是我們兩個人不和[14]，秦國就會來進攻。我躲著廉頗將軍，不是怕他，而是為了我們的國家啊。"

後來，有人告訴了廉頗這些話。廉頗聽了以後，想了很久，知道自己錯了。他就背著一根很粗的荊條，到藺相如家裡去請罪。廉頗見了藺相如就說："我錯了，我太驕傲了。您為了國家，對我這麼好。請您用這根荊條打我吧。"

藺相如趕快把荊條從廉頗背上拿下來，說："廉頗將軍不要這樣。我們兩個人都是趙國的大將軍，應該一起為國家服務。您能夠理解[15]我，我已經很高興了，怎麼還能讓您來給我道歉[16]呢。"

就這樣，他們成了最好的朋友，一起為趙國立了很多功勞。

"負荊請罪"就是說，知道自己錯了，就去向別人道歉。

VOCABULARY LIST

	SIMPLIFIED CHARACTERS	TRADITIONAL CHARACTERS	*PINYIN*	PART OF SPEECH	ENGLISH DEFINITION
1.	负荆	負荊	fù jīng	vo.	to carry a birch
	请罪	請罪	qǐng zuì	vo.	to ask for punishment
2.	廉颇	廉頗	Lián Pō	pn.	name of a person
3.	赵国	趙國	Zhào Guó	pn.	State of Zhao
4.	将军	將軍	jiāngjūn	n.	military general
5.	胜仗	勝仗	shèng zhàng	n.	triumphant battles
6.	立	立	lì	v.	to render
7.	功劳	功勞	gōngláo	n.	meritorious service
8.	骄傲	驕傲	jiāo'ào	adj.	arrogant, proud
9.	蔺相如	藺相如	Lìn Xiāngrú	pn.	name of a person
10.	官	官	guān	n.	government official
11.	躲	躲	duǒ	v.	to hide, to avoid
12.	秦国	秦國	Qín Guó	pn.	State of Qin
13.	可怕	可怕	kěpà	adj.	terrifying
14.	不和	不和	bùhé	adj.	to not get along
15.	理解	理解	lǐjiě	v.	to understand
16.	道歉	道歉	dàoqiàn	v.	to apologize

Bringing a Birch and Begging for a Flogging

QUESTIONS

Reading Comprehension

1. What was Lin Xiangru's position in Zhao?

    A. General

    B. Admiral

    C. Official

    D. Prime minister

2. Why was Lian Po upset with Lin Xiangru?

    A. He thought Lin Xiangru was arrogant and boastful.

    B. Lin Xiangru had been promoted higher than Lian Po.

    C. He thought that Lin Xiangru had lied about his deeds.

    D. The King of Zhao liked Lin Xiangru more than Lian Po.

3. How did Lin Xiangru feel after hearing Lian Po's words?

    A. Cautious

    B. Angry

    C. Afraid

    D. Anxious

4. Why did Lin Xiangru hide from Lian Po?

    A. He was afraid of Lian Po's power.

    B. He was secretly planning to punish Lian Po.

    C. He did it for the good of the country.

    D. He did it for his own reputation.

5. Why did Lian Po ask Lin Xiangru to punish him?

    A. Lian Po realized that the King of Qin was more frightening than Lin Xiangru.

    B. Lian Po realized that Lin Xiangru was a better general than him.

    C. Lian Po felt that he had put his own pride before the country, unlike Lin Xiangru.

    D. Lian Po had said bad things about Lin Xiangru to the King of Zhao.

6. Did Lin Xiangru punish Lian Po?

    A. Yes. He hit Lian Po with a birch.

    B. Yes. He asked Lian Po to apologize in public.

    C. No. However, he did not forgive Lian Po.

    D. No. They managed to make amends.

7. Which reason best explains why a parent or teacher might tell this story to a child?

    A. To introduce the child to the history of Qin and Zhao.

    B. To explain why the child must be punished for misbehavior.

    C. To explain why the child should not be jealous of others.

    D. To show the importance of admitting mistakes and apologizing.

Discussion

1. In your opinion, which of the two historical figures was more admirable? Why?

2. Are there any stories in your own culture that convey a similar lesson?

3. Online, research the countries of Qin and Zhao, and the King of Qin. Why might the people in Zhao be afraid of the King of Qin?

16

CAO CHONG WEIGHS AN ELEPHANT

曹冲称₁象

曹冲稱₁象

Cáo Chōng chēng xiàng

Cao Chong (196–208 C.E.) was a son of Cao Cao, a powerful Chinese warlord, politician, and poet who lived during the Three Kingdoms period (220–280 C.E.). Cao Chong was renowned as a child prodigy and was said to have a mature intelligence by the age of five.

曹冲是曹操,的最小的儿子，他从小就很聪明。

有一次，有人送给曹操一只大象。曹操很高兴，就问他的官员："你们谁知道这只大象有多重,吗？"他们互相看了看，谁也不知道她有多重。

曹操又问他们："你们谁有办法把大象称一称？"这可是太难了。大象是最大的动物。那时候没有那么大的秤,，怎么称呢？官员们围,着大象看来看去，都不知道怎么办。

这时候，一个小孩子跑出来，对大家说："我有办法，我有办法！"大家一看，是曹操的小儿子曹冲，心里就想："大人都想不出办法来，一个五岁的小孩子，会有什么办法？"

他爸爸笑着说："好！你有办法，快说出来给大家听听。"曹冲说："我称给你们看，你们就知道了。"

小曹冲叫人牵,着大象，跟他一起到河边去。他的爸爸，还有那些官员们都想看看他怎么称大象，就也去了河边。

河里有一只大船，曹冲说："把大象牵到船上去。"大象上了船，船就往下沉,了一些。曹冲说："齐,着水面,在船边上做一个记号。"

曹沖是曹操[2]的最小的兒子，他從小就很聰明。

有一次有人送給曹操一隻大象。曹操很高興，就問他的官員："你們誰知道這隻大象有多重[3]嗎？"他們互相看了看，誰也不知道她有多重。

曹操又問他們："你們誰有辦法把大象稱一稱？"這可是太難了。大象是最大的動物。那時候沒有那麼大的秤[4]，怎麼稱呢？官員們圍[5]著大象看來看去，都不知道怎麼辦。

這時候，一個小孩子跑出來，對大家說："我有辦法，我有辦法！"大家一看，是曹操的小兒子曹沖，心裡就想："大人都想不出辦法來，一個五歲的小孩子，會有什麼辦法？"

他爸爸笑著說："好！你有辦法，快說出來給大家聽聽。"曹沖說："我稱給你們看，你們就知道了。"

小曹沖叫人牽[6]著大象，跟他一起到河邊去。他的爸爸，還有那些官員們都想看看他怎麼稱大象，就也去了河邊。

河裡有一隻大船，曹沖說："把大象牽到船上去。"大象上了船，船就往下沉[7]了一些。曹沖說："齊[8]著水面[9]在船邊上做一個記號。"

记号做好了以后，<u>曹冲</u>又叫人把大象牵上岸来。这时候大船空着，大船就往上浮起一些来。大家看着，一会儿把大象牵上船，一会儿又把大象牵下船，心里都说："这孩子在做什么呀？"

　　然后，小<u>曹冲</u>又叫人拿了很多石头，放到船里去，大船又开始慢慢地往下沉了。

　　"好了，好了！"<u>曹冲</u>看见船边上的记号齐水面了，就叫人把石头拿下船来，放在秤上称。

　　大家还是不知道<u>曹冲</u>在做什么，小<u>曹冲</u>笑着说："石头和大象放进船里以后，船边上的记号都齐水面了，那么，石头和大象就是一样重了。如果我们把这些石头都称一称，不就是大象的重量了吗？"

　　大家听了，都夸<u>曹冲</u>，说："这办法听起来虽然简单，可是大人还没想到呢。他年纪这么小，就知道怎样称大象。真是个聪明的好孩子！"

記號做好了以後，曹沖又叫人把大象牽上岸來。這時候大船空著，大船就往上浮$_{10}$起一些來。大家看著，一會兒把大象牽上船，一會兒又把大象牽下船，心裡都說："這孩子在做什麼呀？"

然後，小曹沖又叫人拿了很多石頭，放到船裡去，大船又開始慢慢地往下沉了。

"好了，好了！"曹沖看見船邊上的記號齊水面了，就叫人把石頭拿下船來，放在秤上稱。

大家還是不知道曹沖在做什麼，小曹沖笑著說："石頭和大象放進船裡以後，船邊上的記號都齊水面了，那麼，石頭和大象就是一樣重了。如果我們把這些石頭都稱一稱，不就是大象的重量$_{11}$了嗎？"

大家聽了，都誇曹沖，說："這辦法聽起來雖然簡單$_{12}$，可是大人還沒想到呢。他年紀這麼小，就知道怎樣稱大象。真是個聰明的好孩子！"

VOCABULARY LIST

	SIMPLIFIED CHARACTERS	TRADITIONAL CHARACTERS	*PINYIN*	PART OF SPEECH	ENGLISH DEFINITION
1.	称	稱	chēng	v.	to weigh
2.	曹操	曹操	Cáo Cāo	pn.	name of a person
3.	多重	多重	duōzhòng	n.	how heavy…?
4.	秤	秤	chèng	n.	scale
5.	围	圍	wéi	v.	to surround
6.	牵	牽	qiān	v.	to lead along
7.	沉	沉	chén	v.	to sink
8.	齐	齊	qí	v.	to be on a level with
9.	水面	水面	shuǐmiàn	n.	the water's surface
10.	浮	浮	fú	v.	to float
11.	重量	重量	zhòngliàng	n.	weight
12.	简单	簡單	jiǎndān	adj.	simple

Cao Chong Weighs an Elephant

QUESTIONS

Reading Comprehension

1. Who was Cao Cao?

   A.   Cao Chong's son

   B.   Cao Chong's father

   C.   Cao Chong's uncle

   D.   Cao Chong's brother

2. Cao Cao received the elephant

   A.   from a zoo.

   B.   from a forest.

   C.   from a boat.

   D.   as a gift.

3. What did Cao Cao want to know about the elephant?

   A.   How much it weighed.

   B.   How much space (volume) it took up.

   C.   How many stones it weighed.

   D.   Where it came from.

4. Why were people unable to come up with a solution for Cao Cao?

   A.   They did not want to show off their intelligence.

   B.   There was no scale available.

   C.   There was no scale big enough to weigh the elephant.

   D.   The boat was too small to fit the elephant.

5. Where did Cao Chong ask to make a mark?

   A. On the bank

   B. On the boat

   C. On the elephant

   D. On the rocks

6. What did Cao Chong ask to put on the boat after the elephant?

   A. Another elephant

   B. Water

   C. Rocks

   D. Scales

7. What is the main idea of this story?

   A. Cao Cao's children were all very talented.

   B. Large objects can be weighed using water displacement.

   C. Children often come up with ideas that adults do not think of.

   D. Cao Chong was a very intelligent child.

Discussion

1. Are there any other ways to weigh a heavy object without using a scale?

2. Do you know the story behind the phrase "Eureka!"? How is it similar to and/or different from the story of Cao Chong?

3. Online, research Cao Cao and Cao Chong. When did they live? Why is Cao Cao famous? What happened to Cao Chong, and what did this mean to Cao Cao's family?

17

BREAKING THE WATER VAT TO SAVE A LIFE

司 马 光 砸 缸₁

司 马 光 砸 缸₁

司 馬 光 砸 缸₁

Sīmǎ Guāng zá gāng

Sima Guang (1019–1086 C.E.) was a Chinese historian, scholar, and statesman of the Song dynasty (960–1279 C.E.). He was born to a wealthy family and obtained early success as a scholar and an official, passing the highest scholarly exam when he was only twenty. Today he is still remembered for his great historical work, *Comprehensive Mirror to Aid in Government*.

司马光很小的时候就很喜欢学习。他常常专心$_2$读书，有时候连吃饭喝水都忘记了。司马光不但很喜欢学习，而且还很聪明，勇敢$_3$。有一个故事特别有名，到今天人们都还记得。

司马光七岁的时候，有一次，他跟小朋友们在家里捉迷藏$_4$。他家里放着一口大水缸，水缸里装满$_5$了水。

有一个小朋友快要被捉住$_6$了，就赶快爬到水缸上面去。可是，一不小心，他掉到水缸里去了。

水缸很大，水很深，那孩子在里面又喊$_7$又叫，就要沉下去了。

别的孩子看到了，怕极了，一起大哭起来。有的往外面跑，去找爸爸妈妈来帮忙。

小司马光看到水缸里的孩子快要沉下去了，如果等大人来救$_8$，就会太晚了。他想了想，就从地上找来一块大石头，往水缸上面砸了过去。

只听见"砰$_9$"的一声，水缸被砸破$_{10}$了，缸里的水很快流了出来，掉到缸里的小孩也就救出来了。

小孩的爸爸妈妈知道了这件事情，非常感激$_{11}$司马光，对他说："你真是个聪明勇敢的好孩子，救了我们的儿子。"

直到今天，大家还很佩服$_{12}$他，说他这么小小的年纪就这么聪明勇敢。

司馬光很小的時候就很喜歡學習。他常常專心[2]讀書，有時候連吃飯喝水都忘記了。司馬光不但很喜歡學習，而且還很聰明，勇敢[3]。有一個故事特別有名，到今天人們都還記得。

司馬光七歲的時候，有一次，他跟小朋友們在家裡捉迷藏[4]。他家裡放著一口大水缸，水缸裡裝滿[5]了水。

有一個小朋友快要被捉住[6]了，就趕快爬到水缸上面去。可是，一不小心，他掉到水缸裡去了。

水缸很大，水很深，那孩子在裡面又喊[7]又叫，就要沉下去了。

別的孩子看到了，怕極了，一起大哭起來。有的往外面跑，去找爸爸媽媽來幫忙。

小司馬光看到水缸裡的孩子快要沉下去了，如果等大人來救[8]，就會太晚了。他想了想，就從地上找來一塊大石頭，往水缸上面砸了過去。

只聽見"砰[9]"的一聲，水缸被砸破[10]了，缸裡的水很快流了出來，掉到缸裡的小孩也就救出來了。

小孩的爸爸媽媽知道了這件事情，非常感激[11]司馬光，對他說："你真是個聰明勇敢的好孩子，救了我們的兒子。"

直到今天，大家還很佩服[12]他，說他這麼小小的年紀就這麼聰明勇敢。

VOCABULARY LIST

	SIMPLIFIED CHARACTERS	TRADITIONAL CHARACTERS	*PINYIN*	PART OF SPEECH	ENGLISH DEFINITION
1.	砸	砸	zá	v.	to break with force
	缸	缸	gāng	n.	vat
2.	专心	專心	zhuānxīn	adj.	wholly absorbed
3.	勇敢	勇敢	yǒnggǎn	adj.	brave
4.	捉迷藏	捉迷藏	zhuō mícáng	v.	to play hide-and-seek
5.	装满	裝滿	zhuāng mǎn	vc.	to be fully loaded
6.	捉住	捉住	zhuōzhù	vc.	to be caught
7.	喊	喊	hǎn	v.	to scream
8.	救	救	jiù	v.	to rescue
9.	砰	砰	pēng	on.	the sound of a bang
10.	破	破	pò	v.	to break
11.	感激	感激	gǎnjī	v.	to feel grateful
12.	佩服	佩服	pèifu	v.	to admire

Breaking the Water Vat to Save a Life

QUESTIONS

Reading Comprehension

1. When he was young, Sima Guang liked to

    A.   play games.

    B.   eat and drink.

    C.   study.

    D.   fight other boys.

2. Which trait did Sima Guang not exhibit in the story?

    A.   Studiousness

    B.   Determination

    C.   Intelligence

    D.   Bravery

3. While Sima Guang and his friends were playing,

    A.   Sima Guang accidentally broke a water vat.

    B.   Sima Guang accidentally fell into a water vat.

    C.   one of Sima Guang's friends accidentally broke a water vat.

    D.   one of Sima Guang's friends accidentally fell into a water vat.

4. Why did this happen?

    A.   Sima Guang was afraid of being caught.

    B.   Sima Guang was curious about the water vat.

    C.   One of Sima Guang's friends was afraid of being caught.

    D.   One of Sima Guang's friends was curious about the water vat.

5. What didn't the other kids do?

   A. Be scared

   B. Cry

   C. Ask their parents for help

   D. Look into the water vat

6. Sima Guang did not wait for an adult to come help because

   A. he thought an adult would not care.

   B. he thought an adult would come too late.

   C. he thought an adult would break the water vat.

   D. he thought an adult would punish him.

7. What is the main idea of this story?

   A. Sima Guang was intelligent and brave, even as a child.

   B. Sima Guang's actions as a child proved he would become a great statesman as an adult.

   C. Sima Guang loved to study as a child.

   D. Playing hide and seek without supervision can be dangerous.

Discussion

1. Are there any stories from your own culture that depict a famous person displaying traits or skills as a child that they became famous for as an adult?

2. Online, research Sima Guang. When did he live? What was he famous for?

III

MYTHS AND FANTASIES

第三章 神话故事
第三章 神話故事

18

BIRD JINGWEI FILLS UP THE SEA

精卫填海₁

精衛填海₁

Jīngwèi tián hǎi

传说,很久以前,有一个炎帝,他有一个又聪明又可爱的女儿,叫女娃。炎帝很爱他的女儿,可是他天天很忙,没有时间跟她一起玩儿。女娃就常常自己一个人坐着小船,到各地去玩儿。她去了很多有意思的地方。有一天,她想到很远的地方去看看。可是,这一天海上刮起了大风,下起了大雨,海浪像小山一样,把她的船打翻了。就这样,女娃被大海淹死了,再也回不来了。炎帝很伤心,常常哭着,叫着女儿的名字。

女娃虽然淹死了,可是她的灵魂变成了一只可爱的小鸟。它一边飞,一边叫着,"精卫、精卫,"所以,

傳說$_2$很久以前，有一個炎帝$_3$，他有一個又聰明又可愛的女兒，叫女娃$_4$。炎帝很愛他的女兒，可是他天天很忙，沒有時間跟她一起玩兒。女娃就常常自己一個人坐著小船，到各地去玩兒。她去了很多有意思的地方。有一天，她想到很遠的地方去看看。可是，這一天海上刮起了大風，下起了大雨，海浪$_5$像小山一樣，把她的船打翻$_6$了。就這樣，女娃被大海淹死$_7$了，再也回不來了。炎帝很傷心，常常哭著，叫著女兒的名字。

女娃雖然淹死了，可是她的靈魂$_8$變$_9$成了一隻可愛的小鳥$_{10}$。它一邊飛，一邊叫著，"精衛、精衛，"所以，人們都把它叫做"精衛。"

人们都把它叫做"精卫。"

精卫仇恨[11]大海，因为它淹死了自己，从此不能跟爸爸妈妈在一起了，让爸爸妈妈很伤心。她要报仇[12]，要把大海填平[13]！因此，她找来一粒粒[14]小石头，和一根根[15]小树枝[16]，一直飞到大海，把石子和树枝投[17]下去。她天天这样,飞个不停[18]，一定要把大海填平。

大海笑她，说："小鸟，你那么小，每天投下这么一点点，你投一万年，也不能把我填平啊。"

精卫回答说："一万年，就是一百万年，我也一定要把你填平！"

大海又问："那你为什么一定要把我填平呢？"

精卫说："因为你淹死了我，你以后还会淹死很多别的人，所以我一定要把你填平！"

人们都很佩服精卫，觉得她又坚强[19]又有毅力[20]，一定能成功。

　　精衛仇恨₁₁大海，因為它淹死了自己，從此不能跟爸爸媽媽在一起了，讓爸爸媽媽很傷心。她要報仇₁₂，要把大海填平₁₃！因此，她找來一粒粒₁₄小石頭，和一根根₁₅小樹枝₁₆，一直飛到大海，把石子和樹枝投₁₇下去。她天天這樣，飛個不停₁₈，一定要把大海填平。

　　大海笑她，說：“小鳥，你那麼小，每天投下這麼一點點，你投一萬年，也不能把我填平啊。”

　　精衛回答說：“一萬年，就是一百萬年，我也一定要把你填平！”

　　大海又問：“那你為什麼一定要把我填平呢？”

　　精衛說：“因為你淹死了我，你以後還會淹死很多別的人，所以我一定要把你填平!”

　　人們都很佩服精衛，覺得她又堅強₁₉又有毅力₂₀，一定能成功。

VOCABULARY LIST

	SIMPLIFIED CHARACTERS	TRADITIONAL CHARACTERS	*PINYIN*	PART OF SPEECH	ENGLISH DEFINITION
1.	填	填	tián	v.	to fill up
	海	海	hǎi	n.	sea
2.	传说	傳說	chuánshuō	n.	legend
3.	炎帝	炎帝	Yándì	pn.	Yan Emperor (Yandi)
4.	女娃	女娃	Nǚwá	pn.	name of a person
5.	海浪	海浪	hǎilàng	n.	sea waves
6.	打翻	打翻	dǎfān	v.	to be capsized
7.	淹死	淹死	yānsǐ	v.	to be drowned
8.	灵魂	靈魂	línghún	n.	soul, spirit
9.	变	變	biàn	v.	to change, to transform
10.	鸟	鳥	niǎo	n.	bird
11.	仇恨	仇恨	chóuhèn	v.	to hate
12.	报仇	報仇	bào chóu	vo.	to avenge
13.	填平	填平	tián píng	vc.	to be filled up
14.	粒	粒	lì	mw.	measure word for grains

Bird Jingwei Fills Up the Sea

SIMPLIFIED CHARACTERS	TRADITIONAL CHARACTERS	*PINYIN*	PART OF SPEECH	ENGLISH DEFINITION
15. 根	根	gēn	mw.	measure word for long, slender objects
16. 树枝	樹枝	shùzhī	n.	branch
17. 投	投	tóu	v.	to throw
18. 停	停	tíng	v.	to stop
19. 坚强	堅强	jiānqiáng	adj.	strong
20. 毅力	毅力	yìlì	n.	perseverance

Reading Comprehension

1. What does Nuwa usually do?

   A.   Spend time with her father Yandi.

   B.   Make a small boat by herself.

   C.   See different places by boat.

   D.   Travel to faraway lands.

2. What happened to Nuwa when she went to sea during a storm?

   A.   Her boat was swept out to sea and she never returned.

   B.   Her boat capsized and she drowned.

   C.   Her boat capsized, but her father, Yandi, changed her into a bird.

   D.   She vanished, but returned as a bird.

3. Why was the bird that Nuwa's soul turned into named Jingwei?

   A.   Because Jingwei is a beautiful name.

   B.   Because Jingwei is the former name of Nuwa.

   C.   Because of the bird's appearance.

   D.   Because of the bird's song.

4. What did Jingwei use to try to fill up the sea?

   A.   Pebbles and twigs

   B.   Boulders and large sticks

   C.   Dirt and sand

   D.   Tears

5. The sea considered Jingwei to be

    A.   brave.

    B.   foolish.

    C.   smart.

    D.   determined.

6. Why did Jingwei continue to try to fill up the sea?

    A.   She was afraid of it.

    B.   It kept her from flying far away.

    C.   She did not like water.

    D.   She wanted to prevent other people from drowning.

7. Which reason best explains why a parent or teacher would tell this story to a child?

    A.   To demonstrate true devotion between a daughter and father.

    B.   To explain where beaches come from.

    C.   To make the child afraid of taking a boat out into the ocean.

    D.   To encourage the child to be determined, even when a situation appears impossible.

Discussion

1. Do you think that Jingwei is foolish or admirable? Why?

2. Are there any myths from other cultures about perseverance and impossible tasks? How are they similar to and different from the myth of Jingwei?

3. Online, research some of the legendary emperors of ancient China. What else was the Yan Emperor known for? Who was the Yellow Emperor; what did he do?

19

GODDESS NUWA MENDS THE SKY

女娲补天₁
女媧補天₁

Nǚwā bǔ tiān

传说很久很久以前，中国有一位美丽的女神[2]，她的名字叫<u>女娲</u>。<u>女娲</u>是一位很善良[3]的神，她为人们做了很多好事。她创造[4]了人，又教会他们结婚[5]生孩子。可是，最让人们感动[6]的，是她补天的故事。

有一天，水神[7]和火神[8]打起来了。他们从天上一直打到地下，把天打破了，上面出了一个很大的洞[9]。天破了以后，它很快就塌[10]下来了，地也裂开[11]了，到处都是大火，水也从地下喷[12]出来了。很多人都病了，死了。

<u>女娲</u>看见了，心里很着急，也很伤心。她一定要为人们再做一件大事，那就是把塌下来的天补好！<u>女娲</u>找来了各种颜色的石头，用火把它们变成了石浆[13]，再用这种石浆把天上的洞补好。然后，<u>女娲</u>再用大龟的脚，把塌下来的天支撑[14]起来了。

傳說很久很久以前，中國有一位美麗的女神[2]，她的名字叫女媧。女媧是一位很善良[3]的神，她為人們做了很多好事。她創造[4]了人，又教會他們結婚[5]生孩子。可是，最讓人們感動[6]的，是她補天的故事。

有一天，水神[7]和火神[8]打起來了。他們從天上一直打到地下，把天打破了，上面出了一個很大的洞[9]。天破了以後，它很快就塌[10]下來了，地也裂開[11]了，到處都是大火，水也從地下噴[12]出來了。很多人都病了，死了。

女媧看見了，心裡很著急，也很傷心。她一定要為人們再做一件大事，那就是把塌下來的天補好！女媧找來了各種顏色的石頭，用火把它們變成了石漿[13]，再用這種石漿把天上的洞補好。然後，女媧再用大龜的腳，把塌下來的天支撐[14]起來了。

女娲就这样一直忙着，她先把天补好，再把地填平了，然后又把火和水都停了。人们又可以快乐地生活₁₅了。但是女娲累病了。人们都去看她，为她的病着急。可是，女娲笑着说："我病了没关系，只要我能帮助大家，让你们过得快乐，我就高兴了。"

因此，人们都很感激女娲，希望她的病快点好起来，可是女娲还是病死了。她死了以後，人们常常想着她，感谢她为大家作了那么多好事情。在人们的心中，女娲永远₁₆是一位美丽善良的女神。

女媧就這樣一直忙著，她先把天補好，再把地填平了，然後又把火和水都停了。人們又可以快樂地生活$_{15}$了。但是女媧累病了。人們都去看她，為她的病著急。可是，女媧笑著說:"我病了沒關係，只要我能幫助大家，讓你們過得快樂，我就高興了。"

因此，人們都很感激女媧，希望她的病快點好起來，可是女媧還是病死了。她死了以後，人們常常想著她，感謝她為大家作了那麼多好事情。在人們的心中，女媧永遠$_{16}$是一位美麗善良的女神。

VOCABULARY LIST

	SIMPLIFIED CHARACTERS	TRADITIONAL CHARACTERS	*PINYIN*	PART OF SPEECH	ENGLISH DEFINITION
1.	补	補	bǔ	v.	to mend
	天	天	tiān	n.	sky
2.	女神	女神	nǚshén	n.	goddess
3.	善良	善良	shànliáng	adj.	good and honest, kind-hearted
4.	创造	創造	chuàngzào	v.	to create
5.	结婚	結婚	jiéhūn	v.	to get married
6.	感动	感動	gǎndòng	v.	to be moved, to be touched
7.	水神	水神	shuǐshén	n.	the god of water
8.	火神	火神	huǒshén	n.	the god of fire
9.	洞	洞	dòng	n.	hole
10.	塌	塌	tā	v.	to fall
11.	裂开	裂開	lièkāi	v.	to split open
12.	喷	噴	pēn	v.	to gush
13.	浆	漿	jiāng	n.	thick liquid, paste
14.	支撑	支撐	zhīchēng	v.	to prop up
15.	生活	生活	shēnghuó	v.	to live
16.	永远	永遠	yǒngyuǎn	adv.	everlastingly

Goddess Nuwa Mends the Sky

QUESTIONS

Reading Comprehension

1. Which of these did the Goddess Nuwa not do?

    A. She taught humans how to grow crops.

    B. She created human beings.

    C. She taught humans about marriage and raising children.

    D. She mended the sky after it was broken.

2. Who broke the sky?

    A. Nuwa

    B. The Fire God and the Water God

    C. The Earth God and the Sky God

    D. Humanity

3. What happened after the sky was broken?

    A. Many people died from disease.

    B. Many people died from hunger.

    C. Many people burned to death.

    D. Many people drowned.

4. How did Nuwa feel about people dying?

    A. Sad and exhausted

    B. Worried and sad

    C. Angry and worried

    D. Exhausted and disappointed

5. What did Nuwa use to mend the sky?

    A.   The feet of the Great Turtle

    B.   Fire

    C.   Water

    D.   Stones

6. After she mended the sky, what happened to Nuwa?

    A.   She was exhausted and went to sleep.

    B.   She was angry and punished the gods who had broken the sky.

    C.   She was exhausted and eventually died.

    D.   She became anxious that the sky would break again.

7. What is the main idea of this story?

    A.   Nuwa was a beautiful and kind goddess.

    B.   The ancient Chinese had a great respect for Nuwa.

    C.   Nuwa was so kind-hearted that she sacrificed herself to protect others by mending the sky.

    D.   The sky can be mended with stones.

Discussion

1. Do you know any myths about goddesses from other cultures? How are those goddesses similar to and different from Nuwa?

2. Online, look up the story of how Nuwa created humanity. How is it similar to and different from other myths about the creation of humanity?

20

PANGU CREATES THE UNIVERSE

盘古开天地
盤古開天地

Pángǔ kāi tiāndì

很久很久以前，天和地合₁在一起。宇宙₂就像一个大鸡蛋₃，里面黑黑的，没有上下左右，也没有东南西北。可是，这个鸡蛋里睡着一个大英雄₄，他就是盘古。

盘古在这个大鸡蛋里睡了一万八千年。有一天，他醒₅过来了，往四面看看，可是到处都是黑黑的，什么也看不见。鸡蛋里面不但很黑，而且又闷又热。盘古想站起来，可是鸡蛋包₆着他的身体，他一下都不能动。

盘古觉得很不舒服，他到处摸摸，找到了一把大斧子₇。他用力挥动₈斧子，只听见"砰"的一声，大鸡蛋裂开了，里面轻₉的东西往上升₁₀，变成了天，重的东西，往下掉，变成了地。从那以后，宇宙就不再是一个大鸡蛋了，而是有了天和地。

盘古打开了天和地，他高兴极了。他的头顶₁₁着天，脚踩₁₂着地，支撑着天和地。盘古又高又大，而且每天都长高一丈₁₃。他每长一丈，天就升

很久很久以前，天和地合[1]在一起。宇宙[2]就像一個大雞蛋[3]，裡面黑黑的，沒有上下左右，也沒有東南西北。可是，這個雞蛋裡睡著一個大英雄[4]，他就是<u>盤古</u>。

<u>盤古</u>在這個大雞蛋裡睡了一萬八千年。有一天，他醒[5]過來了，往四面看看，可是到處都是黑黑的，什麼也看不見。雞蛋裡面不但很黑，而且又悶又熱。<u>盤古</u>想站起來，可是雞蛋包[6]著他的身體，他一下都不能動。

<u>盤古</u>覺得很不舒服，他到處摸摸，找到了一把大斧子[7]。他用力揮動[8]斧子，只聽見"砰"的一聲，大雞蛋裂開了，裡面輕[9]的東西往上升[10]，變成了天，重的東西，往下掉，變成了地。從那以後，宇宙就不再是一個大雞蛋了，而是有了天和地。

<u>盤古</u>打開了天和地，他高興極了。他的頭頂[11]著天，腳踩[12]著地，支撐著天和地。<u>盤古</u>又高又大，而且每天都長高一丈[13]。他每長一丈，天就升

高一丈，地也就增厚₁₄一丈。就这样，天变得越来高越高，地也变得越来越厚。

盘古就这样站着，过了一万八千年以后，他累极了，所以躺下来，闭上了眼睛，可是他就再也醒不过来了。盘古死了以后，他的身体变成了高山，血液₁₅变成了大河，毛发₁₆也变成了花草₁₇和树木₁₈。

人们感激盘古打开了天和地，又把自己的身体变成了美丽的山河。所以，在人们的心中，他永远是一个大英雄。

高一丈，地也就增厚₁₄一丈。就這樣，天變得越來高越高，地也變得越來越厚。

　　盤古就這樣站著，過了一萬八千年以後，他累極了，所以躺下來，閉上了眼睛，可是他就再也醒不過來了。盤古死了以後，他的身體變成了高山，血液₁₅變成了大河，毛髮₁₆也變成了花草₁₇和樹木₁₈。

　　人們感激盤古打開了天和地，又把自己的身體變成了美麗的山河。所以，在人們的心中，他永遠是一個大英雄。

VOCABULARY LIST

	SIMPLIFIED CHARACTERS	TRADITIONAL CHARACTERS	*PINYIN*	PART OF SPEECH	ENGLISH DEFINITION
1.	合	合	hé	v.	to join, to combine
2.	宇宙	宇宙	yǔzhòu	n.	universe, cosmos
3.	鸡蛋	雞蛋	jīdàn	n.	egg
4.	英雄	英雄	yīngxióng	n.	hero
5.	醒	醒	xǐng	v.	to wake up
6.	包	包	bāo	v.	to envelop
7.	斧子	斧子	fǔzi	n.	axe, hatchet
8.	挥动	揮動	huīdòng	v.	to brandish
9.	轻	輕	qīng	adj.	light
10.	升	升	shēng	v.	to lift
11.	顶	頂	dǐng	v.	to prop up, to push up
12.	踩	踩	cǎi	v.	to step on
13.	丈	丈	zhàng	mw.	a unit of length equal to 3 1/3 meters
14.	增厚	增厚	zēnghòu	vc.	to become thick
15.	血液	血液	xuèyè	n.	blood
16.	毛发	毛髮	máofà	n.	hair
17.	花草	花草	huācǎo	n.	flowers and grass
18.	树木	樹木	shùmù	n.	trees

Pangu Creates the Universe

QUESTIONS

Reading Comprehension

1. The story begins with a description of

    A. the sky.

    B. the Earth.

    C. the universe.

    D. Pangu, the hero.

2. According to Chinese mythology, what did the universe look like in the beginning?

    A. Total darkness

    B. An egg

    C. The sun

    D. An ocean

3. What did Pangu see when he first woke up?

    A. Total darkness

    B. An egg

    C. The sun

    D. An ocean

4. What implement did Pangu use to break open the universe?

    A. A sword

    B. His fists

    C. A stick

    D. An axe

5. What did Pangu use the implement to do?

   A.   To cut open the egg.

   B.   To hold the sky.

   C.   To mold the earth.

   D.   To defeat enemies.

6. What caused Pangu's death?

   A.   An accident

   B.   An illness

   C.   Exhaustion

   D.   Old age

7. According to Chinese mythology, where do flowers, grass, and trees come from?

   A.   They grew up from Pangu's blood.

   B.   They are made of Pangu's hair.

   C.   They are made of Pangu's body.

   D.   They appeared when the earth and sky were pulled apart.

Discussion

1. How is this creation story similar to or different from creation stories from other cultures?

2. This story is strongly connected to the concept of yin and yang. Online, research what yin and yang are and represent. How is this concept reflected in the story of Pangu?

21

DA YU CONTROLS THE GREAT FLOOD

大 禹 治 水 ₁
大 禹 治 水 ₁

Dà Yú zhì shuǐ

传说很多很多年以前，中国常常发生大水。发大水的时候，人们的房子塌了，田被淹了，很多人也都被淹死了。大禹的父亲跟人们一起，想办法去治这些大水，可是没有成功。大禹长大了以后，觉得一定要像父亲一样，去为大家治水，让人们快乐地生活。

大禹是一个又认真又聪明的人。他治水以前，先想想父亲以前是怎样治水的，然后就自己到很多大河去考察$_2$，看看那里的情况$_3$，再和人们一起讨论$_4$。大禹考察完了以后，对大河的情况作了认真研究$_5$，就带着大家开始治水了。治水的人工作得很认真，也很辛苦，有时候连饭都吃不饱，可还是一直工作到半夜。大禹的腿都累肿$_6$了，但还是不停下来，一直努力地工作。

就这样，大禹跟人们一起努力治水。他工作得太认真了，很多年都没有回家。有好几次他路过自己家的门口，但是没有进去。

第一次大禹路过家门口的时候，他的妻子要生孩子傳說很多很多年以前，中國常常發生大水。發大水的時候，人們的房子塌了，田被淹了，很多人也都被淹死了。大禹的父親跟人們一起，想辦法去治這些大水，可是沒有成功。大禹長大了以後，覺得一定要像父親一樣，去為大家治水，讓人們快樂地生活。

大禹是一個又認真又聰明的人。他治水以前，先想想父親以前是怎樣治水的，然後就自己到很多大河去考察₂，看看那裡的情況₃，再和人們一起討論₄。大禹考察完了以後，對大河的情況作了認真研究₅，就帶著大家開始治水了。治水的人工作得很認真，也很辛苦，有時候連飯都吃不飽，可還是一直工作到半夜。大禹的腿都累腫₆了，但還是不停下來，一直努力地工作。

就這樣，大禹跟人們一起努力治水。他工作得太認真了，很多年都沒有回家。有好幾次他路過自己家的門口，但是沒有進去。

第一次大禹路過家門口的時候，他的妻子要生孩子了，人们都要他进去看一看，可是大禹说:"治水还没有成功，我怎么能回家呢？"第二次路过家门口的时候，大禹怕影响₇治水，还是没有进去。又有一次，大禹的妻子在家门口看见了他，高兴极了，要他回家去看看孩子，可是他还是没有进去。就这样，大禹把他的时间都用来治水了，他的孩子长大了以后，都不认识爸爸了。

十多年以后，大禹治水成功了！大河再也不会发大水了，人们都快快乐乐地生活。大禹还教人们种稻子₈，养鸡养鱼。人们的生活越来越好，大家都很感激大禹。直到今天，人们还常常跟孩子们说大禹治水的故事，要他们长大以后，像他一样认真努力地工作。

了，人們都要他進去看一看，可是大禹說：“治水還沒有成功，我怎麼能回家呢？”第二次路過家門口的時候，大禹怕影響治水，還是沒有進去。又有一次，大禹的妻子在家門口看見了他，高興極了，要他回家去看看孩子，可是他還是沒有進去。就這樣，大禹把他的時間都用來治水了，他的孩子長大了以後，都不認識爸爸了。

十多年以後，大禹治水成功了！大河再也不會發大水了，人們都快快樂樂地生活。大禹還教人們種稻子，養雞養魚。人們的生活越來越好，大家都很感激大禹。直到今天，人們還常常跟孩子們說大禹治水的故事，要他們長大以後，像他一樣認真努力地工作。

VOCABULARY LIST

	SIMPLIFIED CHARACTERS	TRADITIONAL CHARACTERS	*PINYIN*	PART OF SPEECH	ENGLISH DEFINITION
1.	治水	治水	zhìshuǐ	vo.	to control the great flood
2.	考察	考察	kǎochá	v.	to inspect
3.	情况	情況	qíngkuàng	n.	situation, condition
4.	讨论	討論	tǎolùn	v.	to discuss
5.	研究	研究	yánjiū	v.	to study, to research
6.	肿	腫	zhǒng	adj.	swollen
7.	影响	影響	yǐngxiǎng	v.	to affect
8.	稻子	稻子	dàozi	n.	rice, paddy

Da Yu Controls the Great Flood

QUESTIONS

Reading Comprehension

1. What was caught in the flood at the beginning of the story?

   A.   Houses

   B.   Houses and fields

   C.   Houses, fields, and animals

   D.   Houses, fields, and people

2. Da Yu's father

   A.   drowned in a flood.

   B.   tried to control the floods but failed.

   C.   caused the floods.

   D.   had been so busy trying to control the floods that he never came home to see Da Yu.

3. Da Yu's first step to control the floods was to

   A.   begin digging canals.

   B.   inspect the rivers.

   C.   discuss the situation with the people.

   D.   review his father's approach.

4. How many times did Da Yu refuse to enter his home?

   A.   Once

   B.   Twice

   C.   Three times

   D.   Four times

5. Da Yu refused to enter his home because

   A. he fought with his wife.

   B. he did not want to see his children.

   C. he was too tired to go home.

   D. he wanted to get the floods under control.

6. Which of these did Da Yu not teach?

   A. How to educate children

   B. How to grow crops

   C. How to raise chickens

   D. How to raise fish

7. The main idea of this story is that

   A. great floods were common in ancient China.

   B. Chinese people tell their children about Da Yu to teach them about the value of hard work.

   C. Da Yu worked constantly to help control the floods.

   D. Da Yu worked so hard that he never saw his children while they were growing up.

Discussion

1. What values of traditional Chinese culture are reflected in the story of how Da Yu passed by his house without entering? Do you think these values are still reflected in contemporary Chinese culture?

2. Are there any other myths or stories about great floods from other cultures? How are these stories similar to and different from the story of Da Yu?

3. Online, research the story of Da Yu (sometimes known outside of China as "Yu the Great"). What happened to him after he controlled China's floods? Do you think he was a real figure, or only legendary?

22

KUA FU CHASES THE SUN

夸父追日[1]

夸父追日[1]

Kuā Fù zhuī rì

很久很久以前，在中国的北部有一座高山，山上住着很多巨人₂。他们的首领₃最高最大，人很善良，也很勤劳₄勇敢，他的名字叫<u>夸父</u>。

有一年，天气很热很热，太阳像火一样，树木都死了，大河也干了。很多人都热死了，渴死了。<u>夸父</u>看了，心里很难过₅。他抬起头看看天上的太阳，说："太阳太阳，你太坏₆了！我一定要追上你，把你捉住₇，让你听我们的话。"

人们听了，都说："你不能去呀，太阳离我们那么远，你怎么能追得上呢？"还有的人说："对呀，太阳那么远又那么热，你不热死也会累死的。"可是<u>夸父</u>说："为了大家可以快乐地生活，我一定要追上太阳！把它捉

夸父追日 | SIMPLIFIED

很久很久以前，在中國的北部有一座高山，山上住著很多巨人₂。他們的首領₃最高最大，人很善良，也很勤勞₄勇敢，他的名字叫夸父。

有一年，天氣很熱很熱，太陽像火一樣，樹木都死了，大河也幹了。很多人都熱死了，渴死了。夸父看了，心裡很難過₅。他抬起頭看看天上的太陽，說："太陽太陽，你太壞₆了！我一定要追上你，把你捉住₇，讓你聽我們的話。"

人們聽了，都說："你不能去呀，太陽離我們那麼遠，你怎麼能追得上呢？"還有的人說："對呀，太陽那麼遠又那麼熱，你不熱死也會累死的。"可是夸父說："為了大家可以快樂地生活，我一定要追上太陽！把它捉住，讓它聽我們的話！"

住，让它听我们的话！"

夸父手里拿着一根木杖[8]，往着升起的太阳，拼命地[9]跑。他跑过了一片片大树林，爬过了一座座大山，游过了一条条大河，跑了很远很远。

就这样，<u>夸父</u>跑呀跑呀，离太阳越来越近了，最后终于[10]追上了太阳。<u>夸父</u>高兴极了，他高兴地伸出手去，想把太阳捉住。可是太阳太热太热了，<u>夸父</u>捉不住，他自己也觉得又热又渴。他就跑到河边，一口气喝干了河里的水，又往大海跑去，想去那里喝水，可是<u>夸父</u>还没有跑到大海，就在路上渴死了。

<u>夸父</u>死去以前，还想着大家，所以他把手里的木杖往太阳扔[11]了过去。木杖掉下来以后，变成了一大片桃林[12]，每年树上都长很多大桃子，给过路的人们吃，帮他们止[13]渴。

夸父手裡拿著一根木杖[8]，往著升起的太陽，拼命地跑[9]。他跑過了一片片大樹林，爬過了一座座大山，游過了一條條大河，跑了很遠很遠。

就這樣，夸父跑呀跑呀，離太陽越來越近了，最後終於[10]追上了太陽。夸父高興極了，他高興地伸出手去，想把太陽捉住。可是太陽太熱太熱了，夸父捉不住，他自己也覺得又熱又渴。他就跑到河邊，一口氣喝乾了河裡的水，

又往大海跑去，想去那裡喝水，可是夸父還沒有跑到大海，就在路上渴死了。

夸父死去以前，還想著大家，所以他把手裡的木杖往太陽扔[11]了過去。木杖掉下來以後，變成了一大片桃林[12]，每年樹上都長很多大桃子，給過路的人們吃，幫他們止[13]渴。

VOCABULARY LIST

	SIMPLIFIED CHARACTERS	TRADITIONAL CHARACTERS	*PINYIN*	PART OF SPEECH	ENGLISH DEFINITION
1.	追	追	zhuī	v.	to chase after
2.	巨人	巨人	jùrén	n.	giant
3.	首领	首領	shǒulǐng	n.	leader
4.	勤劳	勤勞	qínláo	adj.	hard-working
5.	难过	難過	nánguò	adj.	sad, heartbroken
6.	捉住	捉住	zhuōzhù	vc.	to grasp
7.	木杖	木杖	mùzhàng	n.	cane, stick
8.	拼命地	拼命地	pīnmìng de	adv.	defying death
9.	终于	終於	zhōngyú	adv.	finally
10.	扔	扔	rēng	v.	to throw, to toss
11.	桃林	桃林	táolín	n.	peach orchard
12.	止	止	zhǐ	v.	to stop

QUESTIONS

Reading Comprehension

1. The giants lived in the mountains in which region of China?

   A. The East

   B. The South

   C. The West

   D. The North

2. Which of these events did not happen because of the extreme heat?

   A. The trees died.

   B. The rivers dried up.

   C. The crops dried up.

   D. Many people died.

3. What did the people say to Kua Fu about his plan to catch the sun?

   A. They said that the sun was too far away to catch.

   B. They said that the sun was too high to catch.

   C. They said that the sun was always moving and could not be caught.

   D. They said that he would burn up before he reached the sun.

4. What did Kua Fu take with him when he chased the sun?

   A. A cloth

   B. A peach

   C. Water

   D. A stick

5. What did Kua Fu not pass when he chased the sun?

   A.   Villages

   B.   Forests

   C.   Rivers

   D.   Mountains

6. What happened after Kua Fu died?

   A.   He fell into the sea and became an island.

   B.   His stick became a peach orchard.

   C.   His stick hit the sun and the weather became cool.

   D.   His stick became a giant peach tree.

7. Kua Fu best represents which of these values?

   A.   Intelligence and cunning

   B.   Height and strength

   C.   Determination and courage

   D.   Kindness and honesty

Discussion

1. Are there similar myths dealing with the sun in other cultures? How are they similar to and different from the story of Kua Fu?

2. Online, research the story of Houyi and the Ten Suns. How is this story similar to and different from the story of Kua Fu?

23

THE MAGIC LOTUS LAMP

宝 莲 灯 ₁

寶 蓮 燈 ₁

Bǎolián dēng

中国有一座高山，叫华山。很久很久以前，山上住着一位美丽的女神，她的名字叫三圣母。三圣母₂有一个宝莲灯，她常常用它来给人们看病，大家都很感激她。

　　另外还有一个人也给人们看病，他还常常到华山上来采药₃。他采药的时候，认识了三圣母，他们一起给人们看病。慢慢地，他们相爱了，结婚了。

　　三圣母的哥哥是天上的二郎神₄，他听说自己的妹妹和一个凡人₅结婚了，很生气，一定要把三圣母捉回去。可是，三圣母拿出她的宝莲灯，把他打败₆了。一年后，三圣母生了一个男孩，叫沉香₇。就在大家高高兴兴地庆祝的时候，二郎神进了三圣母的家，把她的宝莲灯偷走₈了。三圣母没有了宝莲灯，就被二郎神打败了，压在了华山下面。

　　十五年以后，小沉香长大了，他又漂亮又聪明，并且学了很多好武艺₉。

　　沉香常常想妈妈，他说："我一定要救出妈妈，让我们一家团圆₁₀。"于是₁₁，他开始往华山走去。有一天，沉香在路上走着，一条巨大的龙₁₂

中國有一座高山，叫華山。很久很久以前，山上住著一位美麗的女神，她的名字叫三聖母。三聖母[2]有一個寶蓮燈，她常常用它來給人們看病，大家都很感激她。

另外還有一個人也給人們看病，他還常常到華山上來採藥[3]。他採藥的時候，認識了三聖母，他們一起給人們看病。慢慢地，他們相愛了，結婚了。

三聖母的哥哥是天上的二郎神[4]，他聽說自己的妹妹和一個凡人[5]結婚了，很生氣，一定要把三聖母捉回去。可是，三聖母拿出她的寶蓮燈，把他打敗[6]了。一年後，三聖母生了一個男孩，叫沉香[7]。就在大家高高興興地慶祝的時候，二郎神進了三聖母的家，把她的寶蓮燈偷走[8]了。三聖母沒有了寶蓮燈，就被二郎神打敗了，壓在了華山下面。

十五年以後，小沉香長大了，他又漂亮又聰明，並且學了很多好武藝[9]。

沉香常常想媽媽，他說：“我一定要救出媽媽，讓我們一家團圓[10]。”於是[11]，他開始往華山走去。有一天，沉香在路上走著，一條巨大的龍[12]

往他飞来。沉香一点都不怕它。他跟巨龙打起来，把它捉住了，并且把它变成了一把很大很长的斧子。沉香高兴极了，笑着说："太好了！我可以用这把斧子打开华山，救出妈妈。"

沉香终于走到了华山，他挥动斧子用力劈₁₃下去，只听见"轰隆₁₄"一声，华山被劈成了两半，沉香救出了妈妈。妈妈见到了他，高兴得又哭又笑。沉香和妈妈又一起找到了二郎神，把他打败了，拿回了宝莲灯。从此，他们一家在一起快乐地生活着，他的爸爸妈妈还跟以前一样，常常给大家看病。

直到今天，如果你去华山，人们还会告诉你，沉香是在哪儿劈山救母的。

往他飛來。沉香一點都不怕它。他跟巨龍打起來，把它捉住了，並且把它變成了一把很大很長的斧子。沉香高興極了，笑著說："太好了！我可以用這把斧子打開華山，救出媽媽。"

　　沉香終於走到了華山，他揮動斧子用力劈[13]下去，只聽見"轟隆[14]"一聲，華山被劈成了兩半，沉香救出了媽媽。媽媽見到了他，高興得又哭又笑。沉香和媽媽又一起找到了二郎神，把他打敗了，拿回了寶蓮燈。從此，他們一家在一起快樂地生活著，他的爸爸媽媽還跟以前一樣，常常給大家看病。

　　直到今天，如果你去華山，人們還會告訴你，沉香是在哪兒劈山救母的。

VOCABULARY LIST

SIMPLIFIED CHARACTERS	TRADITIONAL CHARACTERS	*PINYIN*	PART OF SPEECH	ENGLISH DEFINITION
1. 宝莲灯	寶蓮燈	Bǎolián dēng	pn.	the magic lotus lamp
2. 三圣母	三聖母	Sān Shèngmǔ	pn.	Holy Mother of Mount Hua
3. 采药	採藥	cǎiyào	v.	to gather medicinal herbs
4. 二郎神	二郎神	Èr Láng Shén	pn.	name of a god
5. 凡人	凡人	fánrén	n.	mortal
6. 打败	打敗	dǎbài	vc.	to defeat
7. 沉香	沉香	Chén Xiāng	pn.	name of a person
8. 偷走	偷走	tōuzǒu	vc.	to steal
9. 武艺	武藝	wǔyì	n.	martial arts
10. 团圆	團圓	tuányuán	n.	reunion
11. 于是	於是	yúshì	conj.	therefore
12. 龙	龍	lóng	n.	dragon
13. 劈	劈	pī	v.	to cleave, to split
14. 轰隆	轟隆	hōnglōng	on.	the sound of rumbling

Reading Comprehension

1. Where did San Sheng Mu live?

    A. Under Mount Hua.

    B. On Mount Hua.

    C. At the base of Mount Hua.

    D. Near Mount Hua.

2. What did San Sheng Mu use to treat her patients?

    A. Chinese medicine

    B. Pills

    C. The magic lamp

    D. Martial arts

3. How did San Sheng Mu and her husband meet?

    A. He was her patient.

    B. One of his friends was her patient.

    C. They shared the same patients.

    D. They met when he was gathering medicinal plants.

4. What happened to San Sheng Mu's lamp?

    A. It was stolen by her brother.

    B. It was stolen by her husband.

    C. It was stolen by her patient.

    D. It was lost by her son.

5. Why was San Sheng Mu pinned under the mountain?

   A.   She had married a mortal and angered her brother.

   B.   Her husband had left her after their child was born.

   C.   Her brother had been jealous of her marriage.

   D.   Many of the people she treated had died and, in anger, the people trapped her.

6. Where did Chen Xiang get his axe?

   A.   He took it from the dragon.

   B.   He found it on the road.

   C.   He turned the dragon into the axe.

   D.   He found it at Mount Hua.

7. What is the main idea of this story?

   A.   Mount Hua is an important place in Chinese mythology.

   B.   San Sheng Mu's magic lamp was very powerful.

   C.   San Sheng Mu was trapped by her brother because she married a mortal, but her son grew up and saved her.

   D.   The gods and mortals were forbidden from marrying.

Discussion

1. Are there any similar myths about children rescuing their parents in other cultures? How are they similar to and different from the story of San Sheng Mu and Chen Xiang?

2. Mount Hua is an important place in many Chinese stories and myths. Online, research another important mountain in China and present it to your class. Include its location and at least one story about the mountain.

附录一 拼音课文

APPENDIX:
SIMPLIFIED CHARACTERS WITH *PINYIN*

bá miáo zhù zhǎng
拔 苗 助 长

---

cóng qián, yǒu yī gè nóng mín zhù zài yī gè xiǎo
从 前， 有 一 个 农 民 住 在 一 个 小
cūn zi lǐ。 tā měi tiān zǎo shang hěn zǎo qǐ chuáng
村 子 里。 他 每 天 早 上 很 早 起 床
dào dì lǐ qù gōng zuò, wǎn shang hěn wǎn cái huí
到 地 里 去 工 作， 晚 上 很 晚 才 回
jiā。
家。

yī nián chūn tiān， tā zài dì lǐ xià le zhǒng zi,
一 年 春 天， 他 在 地 里 下 了 种 子，
bù jiǔ jiù zhǎng chū le hé miáo。 tā fēi cháng gāo
不 久 就 长 出 了 禾 苗。 他 非 常 高
xìng， tiān tiān gěi hé miáo jiāo shuǐ， xī wàng tā men
兴， 天 天 给 禾 苗 浇 水， 希 望 它 们
kuài kuài zhǎng gāo。 tā hái měi tiān dōu yòng yī bǎ
快 快 长 高。 他 还 每 天 都 用 一 把
chǐ zi qù liàng zhè xiē hé miáo， kàn kàn tā men
尺 子 去 量 这 些 禾 苗， 看 看 它 们
zhǎng gāo le duō shǎo。 shí jǐ tiān guò qu le， tā
长 高 了 多 少。 十 几 天 过 去 了， 他
jué de hé miáo zhǎng de tài màn le， hěn zháo jí。
觉 得 禾 苗 长 得 太 慢 了， 很 着 急。
tā xiǎng: "zěn yàng cái néng ràng zhè xiē hé miáo zhǎng
他 想： "怎 样 才 能 让 这 些 禾 苗 长
de kuài yī diǎn ne? "
得 快 一 点 呢? "

tā xiǎng a xiǎng a， xiǎng chū le yī gè bàn fǎ:
他 想 啊 想 啊， 想 出 了 一 个 办 法:
rú guǒ wǒ bǎ zhè xiē hé miáo dōu wǎng shàng bá
"如 果 我 把 这 些 禾 苗 都 往 上 拔

高 一 点 儿, 它 们 不 就 都 长 高 了
吗?" 他 很 快 跑 到 地 里, 把 所 有 的
禾 苗 都 拔 高 了 一 点 儿。

他 拔 到 半 夜 才 回 家。 虽 然 很 累,
但 是 很 高 兴。 他 告 诉 儿 子 说: 我
今 天 帮 助 地 里 的 禾 苗 长 高 了!"
他 的 儿 子 到 地 里 一 看, 却 发 现
所 有 的 禾 苗 都 死 了。

2 . SITTING BY A STUMP TO WAIT FOR A CARELESS HARE

守 株 待 兔

很 久 以 前, 有 一 个 农 民 在 很 远
的 地 方 种 了 一 块 地。 地 的 旁 边
有 一 个 树 桩, 树 桩 旁 边 长 满 了
野 草, 如 果 不 仔 细 看 的 话, 就 看
不 出 里 面 有 一 个 树 桩。 有 时 这
个 农 民 累 了, 就 坐 在 树 桩 上 休
息。

有一天，这个农民正在工作，一只野兔飞一样地从远处跑过来。这只野兔因为跑得太快，没有看到野草里的树桩，一头撞在树桩上，就昏过去了。农民看见了，马上拾起野兔。他非常高兴，心里想："要是每天都有一只野兔从这里跑过，并且撞在这个树桩上，那我为什么还要辛辛苦苦地工作呢？"

从这天以后，这个农民再也不去工作了。他每天早上都来到地里，坐在离树桩不远的地方等着，希望还会有野兔跑过来撞在那儿。

农夫等啊，等啊，一天、两天、三天，很多天过去了，他的地里已经长满了野草。虽然还常有野兔

cóng　dì　biān　pǎo　guò,　kě　shì　méi　yǒu　yī　zhī　zhèng
从　地　边　跑　过,　可　是　没　有　一　只　正

hǎo　zhuàng　zài　nà　gè　shù　zhuāng　shàng。　zuì　hòu,　tā　lián
好　撞　在　那　个　树　桩　上。　最　后,　他　连

chī　fàn　de　qián　dōu　méi　yǒu　le,　chéng　le　rén　men
吃　饭　的　钱　都　没　有　了,　成　了　人　们

de　xiào　huà。
的　笑　话。

3. DRAWING A SNAKE AND ADDING FEET

huà　shé　tiān　zú
画　蛇　添　足

---

hěn　jiǔ　yǐ　qián,　yǒu　yī　gè　fù　rén　jiā,　lǐ　yǒu
很　久　以　前,　有　一　个　富　人,　家　里　有

hěn　duō　pú　rén。　yǒu　yī　tiān,　tā　gěi　le　tā　men
很　多　仆　人。　有　一　天,　他　给　了　他　们

yī　píng　jiǔ。　zhè　jiǔ　hǎo　xiāng　a　kě　shì,　zhǐ　yǒu
一　瓶　酒。　这　酒　好　香　啊!　可　是,　只　有

yī　píng,　pú　rén　què　yǒu　shí　jǐ　gè。　zěn　me　bàn
一　瓶,　仆　人　却　有　十　几　个。　怎　么　办

ne?　zhè　shí,　yǒu　yī　gè　pú　rén　shuō:　"jiǔ　tài　shǎo
呢?　这　时,　有　一　个　仆　人　说:　"酒　太　少

le,　zhǐ　gòu　yī　gè　rén　hē,　ràng　wǒ　men　lái　yī
了,　只　够　一　个　人　喝,　让　我　们　来　一

chǎng　bǐ　sài　ba。　wǒ　men　měi　gè　rén　dōu　yòng　bǐ
场　比　赛　吧。　我　们　每　个　人　都　用　笔

zài　dì　shang　huà　yī　tiáo　shé,　shéi　xiān　huà　hǎo,　zhè
在　地　上　画　一　条　蛇,　谁　先　画　好,　这

píng　jiǔ　jiù　ràng　tā　yī　gè　rén　hē,　hǎo　bù　hǎo?"
瓶　酒　就　让　他　一　个　人　喝,　好　不　好?"

dà　jiā　dōu　shuō　hǎo。
大　家　都　说　好。

rán　hòu,　tā　men　dōu　ná　hǎo　le　bǐ,　yī、　èr、　sān,
然　后,　他　们　都　拿　好　了　笔,　一、　二、　三,

kāi shǐ dà jiā tóng shí zài dì shang huà qǐ shé
开 始! 大 家 同 时 在 地 上 画 起 蛇

lái yǒu yī gè rén hěn kuài jiù huà hǎo le tā
来。 有 一 个 人 很 快 就 画 好 了。 他

kàn jiàn qí tā de rén hái zài huà zhe jiù shuō
看 见 其 他 的 人 还 在 画 着, 就 说:

nǐ men huà de zhēn màn nǐ men kàn wǒ zǎo jiù
"你 们 画 得 真 慢! 你 们 看, 我 早 就

huà wán le zhè jiǔ shì wǒ de le tā bǎ jiǔ
画 完 了! 这 酒 是 我 的 了。" 他 把 酒

ná guò lai yòu kàn le kàn qí tā de rén xiào
拿 过 来, 又 看 了 看 其 他 的 人, 笑

zhe shuō nǐ men hái zài huà ne nà wǒ zài gěi
着 说: "你 们 还 在 画 呢, 那 我 再 给

wǒ de shé huà sì zhī jiǎo ba tā yī biān shuō
我 的 蛇 画 四 只 脚 吧!" 他 一 边 说,

yī biān zài huà hǎo de shé shàng yòu huà le sì
一 边 在 画 好 的 蛇 上 又 画 了 四

zhī jiǎo
只 脚。

kě shì hái méi děng tā bǎ jiǎo huà hǎo dì èr
可 是, 还 没 等 他 把 脚 画 好, 第 二

gè rén yǐ jīng huà wán le zhè gè rén mǎ shàng
个 人 已 经 画 完 了。 这 个 人 马 上

cóng tā shǒu lǐ bǎ jiǔ qiǎng guò lai shuō wǒ men
从 他 手 里 把 酒 抢 过 来, 说: "我 们

bǐ sài huà shé kě shì shé méi yǒu jiǎo a xiàn
比 赛 画 蛇, 可 是 蛇 没 有 脚 啊! 现

zài nǐ què gěi tā huà shàng le jiǎo nà hái néng
在 你 却 给 它 画 上 了 脚, 那 还 能

jiào shé ma xiàn zài wǒ shì dì yī gè huà wán
叫 蛇 吗? 现 在 我 是 第 一 个 画 完

shé de rén le suǒ yǐ zhè píng jiǔ yīng gāi shì
蛇 的 人 了, 所 以 这 瓶 酒 应 该 是

wǒ de shuō wán tā jiù kāi shǐ hē qǐ lai dì
我 的!" 说 完 他 就 开 始 喝 起 来。 第

yī gè huà wán shé de rén fēi cháng shēng qì kě
一 个 画 完 蛇 的 人 非 常 生 气, 可

shì	yī	jù	huà	yě	shuō	bù	chū	lai	yīn	wèi	zhè
是	一	句	话	也	说	不	出	来,	因	为	这

shì	tā	zì	jǐ	guò	cuò	a
是	他	自	己	过	错	啊!

4. MISTAKING THE REFLECTION OF A BOW FOR A SNAKE

bēi	gōng	shé	yǐng
杯	弓	蛇	影

---

zhōng	guó	gǔ	dài	yǒu	yī	gè	rén	jiào	yuè	guǎng	yuè
中	国	古	代	有	一	个	人	叫	乐	广。	乐

guǎng	yǒu	hěn	duō	péng	you	tā	zuì	xǐ	huān	zuò	de
广	有	很	多	朋	友,	他	最	喜	欢	做	的

shì	qíng	jiù	shì	qǐng	tā	de	péng	you	men	dào	jiā
事	情	就	是	请	他	的	朋	友	们	到	家

lǐ	lái	hē	jiǔ	liáo	tiānr		
里	来	喝	酒,	聊	天	儿。	

yǒu	yī	tiān	yuè	guǎng	de	yī	gè	hǎo	péng	you	dào
有	一	天,	乐	广	的	一	个	好	朋	友	到

tā	jiā	lái	le	liǎng	gè	rén	yī	biān	hē	jiǔ	yī
他	家	来	了,	两	个	人	一	边	喝	酒,	一

biān	liáo	tiān	zhèng	dāng	tā	men	liáo	de	hěn	gāo	xìng
边	聊	天。	正	当	他	们	聊	得	很	高	兴

de	shí	hòu	tā	de	péng	you	què	tuī	kāi	jiǔ	bēi
的	时	候,	他	的	朋	友	却	推	开	酒	杯,

shuō	zì	jǐ	de	dù	zi	bù	shū	fu	rán	hòu	jiù
说	自	己	的	肚	子	不	舒	服,	然	后	就

jí	jí	máng	máng	de	huí	jiā	qù	le	yuè	guǎng	jué
急	急	忙	忙	地	回	家	去	了。	乐	广	觉

de	fēi	cháng	qí	guài	hěn	xiǎng	zhī	dào	wèi	shén	me
得	非	常	奇	怪,	很	想	知	道	为	什	么。

dì	èr	tiān	yuè	guǎng	dào	péng	you	jiā	qù	fā	xiàn
第	二	天,	乐	广	到	朋	友	家	去,	发	现

tā	tǎng	zài	chuáng	shàng	hǎo	xiàng	bìng	de	hěn	zhòng	yuè
他	躺	在	床	上,	好	像	病	得	很	重。	乐

广 问:"你 今 天 怎 么 样?"朋 友 说:"我
生 病 了。"乐 广 问:"什 么 病 呢?"朋 友
说:"昨 天 我 在 你 家 里 喝 酒 的 时
候,看 见 一 条 小 蛇 在 我 的 酒 杯
里,我 觉 得 恶 心,可 是 我 还 是 喝
下 去 了。我 一 喝 下 去,就 觉 得 肚
子 很 不 舒 服,回 家 就 生 病 了。"

乐 广 想:"我 家 的 酒 里 怎 么 会 有
蛇 呢?"回 家 以 后,他 坐 在 朋 友 的
座 位 上,并 且 在 面 前 放 了 一 杯
酒。他 一 看 酒 杯 里 面 真 的 有 一
条 小 蛇!这 是 怎 么 回 事 呢?乐 广
抬 头 一 看,原 来 座 位 旁 边 的 墙
上 挂 着 一 张 弓,那 张 弓 的 影 子
映 在 酒 杯 里,就 好 象 是 一 条 小
蛇。

乐 广 马 上 回 到 朋 友 那 儿,请 朋
友 再 到 自 己 家 来。乐 广 请 他 坐
在 原 来 的 座 位 上,又 给 他 倒 了

一杯酒。朋友一看酒杯，吓得大
叫起来："蛇！蛇！"乐广哈哈大笑，慢
慢地站起来，把挂在墙上的弓
拿掉。这时朋友再看酒杯，发现
酒杯里的蛇不见了。原来酒杯
里根本没有小蛇！朋友的"病"一
下子就好了，肚子也不疼了。

5. SIX BLIND MEN AND AN ELEPHANT

盲人摸象

在很远的地方，有一个城市，那
儿住着六个盲人。这六个盲
是好朋友，他们常常在一起聊
天儿。有一天，他们听说有人从
很远的地方带回一只很大
的动物，叫大象。因为谁都没有
见过这种动物，所以大家都去
看它。

这些盲人也很想知道大象是什么样子。虽然他们看不见,可是可以用手摸啊!所以他们也来到大象面前,都用手去摸一摸,然后说说它的样子。

第一个盲人摸到了大象的鼻子,他说:"哦,原来大象是一条圆圆的、粗粗的、长长的管子啊!"

第二个盲人摸到了大象的耳朵,他说:"不对,大象是一把大扇子,搧起风来可凉快呢!"

第三个盲人摸到了大象的身体,他说:"你们都错了,大象是一堵又高又大的墙!"

第四个盲人摸到了大象的腿,他说:"你们说什么呀,大象是一根又粗又圆的大柱子啊!"

第五个盲人摸到了大象的尾

bā tā shuō nǐ men dōu bú duì dà xiàng zhǐ shì
巴, 他 说: "你 们 都 不 对, 大 象 只 是

yī tiáo cháng cháng de shéng zi
一 条 长 长 的 绳 子。"

dì liù gè máng rén mō dào le dà xiàng de yá
第 六 个 盲 人 摸 到 了 大 象 的 牙

chǐ tā shuō wǒ jué de dà xiàng bù cháng yě bù
齿, 他 说: "我 觉 得 大 象 不 长 也 不

duǎn mō qǐ lai hěn guāng huá
短, 摸 起 来 很 光 滑。"

liù gè máng rén dōu jué de zhǐ yǒu zì jǐ cái
六 个 盲 人 都 觉 得 只 有 自 己 才

shì duì de shéi yě bù ràng shéi zhè shí rén men
是 对 的, 谁 也 不 让 谁。这 时, 人 们

xiào zhe duì tā men shuō nǐ men měi gè rén dōu
笑 着 对 他 们 说: "你 们 每 个 人 都

shuō duì le dàn yòu méi yǒu yī gè rén quán duì
说 对 了, 但 又 没 有 一 个 人 全 对。

yīn wèi nǐ men dōu zhǐ mō dào le dà xiàng de
因 为 你 们 都 只 摸 到 了 大 象 的

yī bù fēn bìng méi yǒu mō dào dà xiàng de quán
一 部 分, 并 没 有 摸 到 大 象 的 全

bù
部!"

6. SELF-CONTRADICTION

zì xiāng máo dùn
自 相 矛 盾

---

hěn jiǔ yǐ qián zhōng guó fēn chéng le jǐ gè xiǎo
很 久 以 前, 中 国 分 成 了 几 个 小

guó zhè xiē xiǎo guó cháng cháng dǎ zhàng
国, 这 些 小 国 常 常 打 仗。

nà shí hòu rén men dǎ zhàng yòng de wǔ qì shì
那 时 候, 人 们 打 仗 用 的 武 器 是

máo hé dùn máo shì yòng lái jìn gōng de yǒu cháng
矛 和 盾。矛 是 用 来 进 攻 的, 有 长

长的木柄，木柄的一头装着锋利的矛头，又叫长矛。盾是用来防卫的，用坚硬的金属做成的，打仗时用它挡住身体，可以保护自己不受长矛的攻击。

一天，有一个人在市场上卖武器。他卖的就是矛和盾。他把矛放在一边，又把盾放在另外一边，等到买武器的人来了，他就开始叫卖。

他先拿起一枝矛，对大家说："你们看，我的长矛矛头又锋利又坚硬，不论多么坚硬的盾它都能刺穿！"然后，他又拿起一面盾，对大家说："再来看看我的盾。我的盾是用最坚固的金属做成的，不论多么锋利的长矛都不能把它刺穿！"

大 家 看 看 他 的 矛, 再 看 看 他 的

盾, 觉 得 都 不 错。 这 时 有 一 个 买

武 器 的 人 说:"如 果 我 买 你 的 矛,

再 买 你 的 盾, 然 后 用 你 的 矛 去

刺 你 的 盾, 请 问 会 怎 样 呢?"

这 个 卖 武 器 的 人 一 听, 不 知 道

怎 么 回 答, 只 好 收 起 矛 和 盾 回

家 了。 后 来, 人 们 把 两 种 互 相 对

立 的 情 况 叫 做 矛 盾。 如 果 一 个

人 说 话 前 后 不 一 致, 就 叫 做 "自

相 矛 盾"。

7. A FROG IN A WELL

井 底 之 蛙

很 久 以 前, 在 离 东 海 很 远 的 地

方 有 一 口 井。 这 口 井 很 小, 里 面

住 着 一 只 小 青 蛙。 这 只 青 蛙 一

直 住 在 这 里, 它 去 过 的 最 远 的

地 方 就 是 井 台。

每天早上，青蛙在井里找些小虫吃。早饭以后，它跳出来，在井台上晒晒太阳，然后回到井里去休息。吃过午饭以后，它在井里游泳，玩儿。吃完晚饭以后，它坐在井里，看看天上的星星，然后回去睡觉。它的日子就这样一天一天地过去，它觉得自己过得很快乐。

有一天，青蛙正在井台上玩儿，路上来了一只大海龟。它问大海龟："你的家在哪儿？你是从哪来的？要上哪儿去？"海龟说："我的家在东海。我从东海来，还要回东海去。"青蛙说："东海是什么地方？你为什么要回那儿去呢？像我这样住在井里多好啊！你看，我每天生活得又快乐又舒服。如果你跟我一起住在这儿，

nǐ jiù zài yě bù xiǎng huí dōng hǎi qù le。"
你 就 再 也 不 想 回 东 海 去 了。"

dà hǎi guī tīng jiàn qīng wā bǎ tā de jǐng shuō
大 海 龟 听 见 青 蛙 把 它 的 井 说

de nà me hǎo, jiù xiǎng xià qù kàn kàn, kě shì
得 那 么 好, 就 想 下 去 看 看, 可 是

tā wǎng jǐng lǐ yī kàn, lǐ miàn hēi hēi de, shén
它 往 井 里 一 看, 里 面 黑 黑 的,什

me yě kàn bù jiàn, jǐng kǒu yě tài xiǎo, tóu hé
么 也 看 不 见, 井 口 也 太 小, 头 和

jiǎo dōu shēn bù jìn qù, gèng bù yòng shuō shēn tǐ
脚 都 伸 不 进 去, 更 不 用 说 身 体

le。
了。

dà hǎi guī yáo yáo tóu, duì qīng wā shuō:"xiè xiè
大 海 龟 摇 摇 头, 对 青 蛙 说:"谢 谢

nǐ。 wǒ bù xià qù le。 suī rán nǐ de jǐng hěn
你。 我 不 下 去 了。 虽 然 你 的 井 很

shū fú, wǒ hái shì xǐ huān wǒ de dōng hǎi。 nǐ
舒 服, 我 还 是 喜 欢 我 的 东 海。 你

zhī dào dōng hǎi yǒu duō dà ma? tā fāng yuán yǒu
知 道 东 海 有 多 大 吗? 它 方 圆 有

jǐ qiān lǐ, wǒ men kàn bù dào tā de biān。 nǐ
几 千 里, 我 们 看 不 到 它 的 边。 你

zhī dào dōng hǎi yǒu duō shēn ma? tā yǒu hǎo jǐ
知 道 东 海 有 多 深 吗? 它 有 好 几

lǐ shēn hǎi lǐ yǒu hěn duō dòng wù, wǒ men tiān
里 深,海 里 有 很 多 动 物,我 们 天

tiān zài yī qǐ wánr儿。 zhǐ yǒu zhù zài nàr 儿,
天 在 一 起 玩 儿。 只 有 住 在 那 儿,

wǒ cái jué de zhēn zhèng de kuài lè!"
我 才 觉 得 真 正 地 快 乐!"

qīng wā tīng le dà hǎi guī de huà, cái zhī dào
青 蛙 听 了 大 海 龟 的 话, 才 知 道

jǐng wài miàn hái yǒu nà me dà de shì jiè, jué
井 外 面 还 有 那 么 大 的 世 界, 觉

de 得	zì 自	jǐ 己	zhī 知	dào 道	de 得	tài 太	shǎo 少	le 了,	ér 而	qiě 且	zài 在
yī 一	gè 个	zhī 知	dào 道	de 得	hěn 很	duō 多	de 的	rén 人	miàn 面	qián 前	chuī 吹
niú 牛,	zhēn 真	shì 是	kě 可	xiào 笑。							

8. THREE IN THE MORNING AND FOUR IN THE EVENING

zhāo 朝　sān 三　mù 暮　sì 四

---

cóng 从	qián 前,	yǒu 有	yī 一	wèi 位	lǎo 老	rén 人,	zhù 住	zài 在	yī 一	zuò 座	dà 大
shān 山	páng 旁	biān 边,	shān 山	lǐ 里	yǒu 有	hěn 很	duō 多	hóu 猴	zi 子。	lǎo 老	rén 人
fēi 非	cháng 常	xǐ 喜	huān 欢	zhè 这	xiē 些	hóu 猴	zi 子,	tā 他	cháng 常	cháng 常	zài 在
xiū 休	xi 息	de 的	shí 时	hòu 候	kàn 看	zhe 着	tā 它	men 们	tiào 跳	lái 来	tiào 跳
qù 去,	gāo 高	gāo 高	xìng 兴	xìng 兴	de 地	wánr 玩	儿。	màn 慢	màn 慢	de 地,	zhè 这
xiē 些	hóu 猴	zi 子	dōu 都	hé 和	lǎo 老	rén 人	shóu 熟	xī 悉	qǐ 起	lai 来,	yī 一
diǎnr 点	儿	yě 也	bù 不	pà 怕	tā 他,	hái 还	cháng 常	cháng 常	pǎo 跑	dào 到	tā 他
de 的	shēn 身	biān 边,	gēn 跟	tā 他	yī 一	qǐ 起	wánr 玩	儿。	jiù 就	zhè 这	yàng 样,
lǎo 老	rén 人	hé 和	hóu 猴	zi 子	men 们	chéng 成	le 了	hǎo 好	péng 朋	you 友。	
hòu 后	lái 来,	lǎo 老	rén 人	zài 在	zì 自	jǐ 己	jiā 家	lǐ 里	yǎng 养	le 了	jǐ 几
zhī 只	hóu 猴	zi 子。	lǎo 老	rén 人	hé 和	hóu 猴	zi 子	tiān 天	tiān 天	zài 在	yī 一
qǐ 起,	hù 互	xiāng 相	dōu 都	hěn 很	liǎo 了	jiě 解。	lǎo 老	rén 人	duì 对	hóu 猴	zi 子

<table>
<tr><td>shuō
说</td><td>shén
什</td><td>me
么，</td><td>tā
它</td><td>men
们</td><td>dōu
都</td><td>néng
能</td><td>tīng
听</td><td>dǒng
懂</td><td>tā
他</td><td>yě
也</td><td>néng
能</td></tr>
<tr><td>kàn
看</td><td>chū
出</td><td>tā
它</td><td>men
们</td><td>xiǎng
想</td><td>shuō
说</td><td>shén
什</td><td>me
么。</td></tr>
</table>

<table>
<tr><td>dōng
冬</td><td>tiān
天</td><td>lái
来</td><td>le
了，</td><td>lǎo
老</td><td>rén
人</td><td>gěi
给</td><td>hóu
猴</td><td>zi
子</td><td>men
们</td><td>zhǔn
准</td><td>bèi
备</td></tr>
<tr><td>le
了</td><td>yī
一</td><td>xiē
些</td><td>guǒ
果</td><td>zi
子，</td><td>dàn
但</td><td>shì
是</td><td>tài
太</td><td>shǎo
少</td><td>le
了。</td><td>rú
如</td><td>guǒ
果</td></tr>
<tr><td>tā
它</td><td>men
们</td><td>měi
每</td><td>tiān
天</td><td>néng
能</td><td>shǎo
少</td><td>chī
吃</td><td>jǐ
几</td><td>gè
个，</td><td>hái
还</td><td>kě
可</td><td>yǐ
以</td></tr>
<tr><td>chī
吃</td><td>dào
到</td><td>dì
第</td><td>èr
二</td><td>nián
年</td><td>chūn
春</td><td>tiān
天；</td><td>rú
如</td><td>guǒ
果</td><td>bù
不</td><td>shěng
省</td><td>zhe
着</td></tr>
<tr><td>diǎnr
点儿，</td><td></td><td>guǒ
果</td><td>zi
子</td><td>jiù
就</td><td>huì
会</td><td>bú
不</td><td>gòu
够</td><td>chī
吃。</td><td>tā
他</td><td>suàn
算</td><td>le
了</td></tr>
<tr><td>yī
一</td><td>xià
下，</td><td>měi
每</td><td>zhī
只</td><td>hóu
猴</td><td>zi
子</td><td>měi
每</td><td>tiān
天</td><td>zhǐ
只</td><td>néng
能</td><td>chī
吃</td><td>qī
七</td></tr>
<tr><td>gè
个</td><td>guǒ
果</td><td>zi
子。</td></tr>
</table>

<table>
<tr><td>tā
他</td><td>xiān
先</td><td>gěi
给</td><td>hóu
猴</td><td>zi
子</td><td>men
们</td><td>kàn
看</td><td>le
了</td><td>kàn
看</td><td>guǒ
果</td><td>zi
子，</td><td>rán
然</td></tr>
<tr><td>hòu
后</td><td>duì
对</td><td>tā
它</td><td>men
们</td><td>shuō
说：</td><td>guǒ
"果</td><td>zi
子</td><td>bú
不</td><td>gòu
够</td><td>le
了</td><td>cóng
从</td><td>jīn
今</td></tr>
<tr><td>tiān
天</td><td>qǐ
起，</td><td>nǐ
你</td><td>men
们</td><td>měi
每</td><td>tiān
天</td><td>měi
每</td><td>rén
人</td><td>zhǐ
只</td><td>néng
能</td><td>chī
吃</td><td>qī
七</td></tr>
<tr><td>gè
个</td><td>guǒ
果</td><td>zi
子。"</td><td>hóu
猴</td><td>zi
子</td><td>men
们</td><td>dōu
都</td><td>diǎn
点</td><td>tóu
头</td><td>tóng
同</td><td>yì
意</td><td>le
了。</td></tr>
</table>

<table>
<tr><td>lǎo
老</td><td>rén
人</td><td>yòu
又</td><td>shuō
说：</td><td>wǒ
"我</td><td>měi
每</td><td>tiān
天</td><td>zǎo
早</td><td>shang
上</td><td>gěi
给</td><td>nǐ
你</td><td>men
们</td></tr>
<tr><td>sān
三</td><td>gè
个，</td><td>wǎn
晚</td><td>shang
上</td><td>gěi
给</td><td>nǐ
你</td><td>men
们</td><td>sì
四</td><td>gè
个，</td><td>hǎo
好</td><td>bù
不</td><td>hǎo
好？"</td></tr>
<tr><td>hóu
猴</td><td>zi
子</td><td>men
们</td><td>yī
一</td><td>tīng
听，</td><td>dōu
都</td><td>hěn
很</td><td>bù
不</td><td>gāo
高</td><td>xìng
兴，</td><td>gè
个</td><td>gè
个</td></tr>
<tr><td>yáo
摇</td><td>tóu
头</td><td>bù
不</td><td>tóng
同</td><td>yì
意，</td><td>jué
觉</td><td>de
得</td><td>zǎo
早</td><td>shang
上</td><td>zhǐ
只</td><td>chī
吃</td><td>sān
三</td></tr>
<tr><td>gè
个</td><td>guǒ
果</td><td>zi
子</td><td>tài
太</td><td>shǎo
少</td><td>le
了。</td><td>lǎo
老</td><td>rén
人</td><td>yòu
又</td><td>shuō
说：</td><td>nà
"那</td><td>me
么</td></tr>
</table>

zǎo shang sì gè, wǎn shang sān gè, zěn me yàng?" hóu
早 上 四 个， 晚 上 三 个， 怎 么 样？" 猴

zi men yī tīng zǎo shang duō le yī gè guǒ zi,
子 们 一 听 早 上 多 了 一 个 果 子，

dōu hěn gāo xìng, yòu jiào yòu tiào, yī diǎnr yì
都 很 高 兴， 又 叫 又 跳， 一 点 儿 意

jiàn yě méi yǒu le.
见 也 没 有 了。

9. CARVING A MARK ON A BOAT

TO LOOK FOR A LOST SWORD

kè zhōu qiú jiàn
刻 舟 求 剑

---

cóng qián, yǒu yī gè rén zuò chuán qù bàn shì tā
从 前， 有 一 个 人 坐 船 去 办 事 他

shēn shàng dài zhe yī bǎ bǎo jiàn. dāng chuán dào le
身 上 带 着 一 把 宝 剑。 当 船 到 了

jiāng xīn de shí hòu, tā de jiàn bù xiǎo xīn diào
江 心 的 时 候， 他 的 剑 不 小 心 掉

dào jiāng lǐ qù le. chuán shàng de rén dōu wèi tā
到 江 里 去 了。 船 上 的 人 都 为 他

zháo jí, jué de zhè tài kě xī le, jiào tā gǎn
着 急， 觉 得 这 太 可 惜 了， 叫 他 赶

kuài tiào dào shuǐ lǐ qù lāo.
快 跳 到 水 里 去 捞。

kě shì zhè gè rén què yī diǎnr yě bù zháo
可 是 这 个 人 却 一 点 儿 也 不 着

jí. tā ná chū yī bǎ xiǎo dāo, zài zì jǐ de
急。 他 拿 出 一 把 小 刀， 在 自 己 的

zuò wèi páng biān kè le yī gè jì hào, rán hòu
座 位 旁 边 刻 了 一 个 记 号， 然 后

duì dà jiā shuō: "méi guān xì, wǒ zài zhèr kè
对 大 家 说："没 关 系， 我 在 这 儿 刻

shàng jì hào le, děng chuán dào le duì àn, wǒ zhǐ
上 记 号 了， 等 船 到 了 对 岸， 我 只

要 从 这 个 有 记 号 的 地 方 跳 下
去, 就 可 以 找 到 我 的 剑 了。"
船 到 了 岸 以 后, 这 个 人 就 从 那
个 有 记 号 的 地 方 跳 到 江 里, 去
捞 他 的 宝 剑, 可 是 什 么 也 没 有
捞 到。

有 一 个 老 人 对 他 说:"年 轻 人! 虽
然 你 的 宝 剑 掉 下 去 的 时 候 你
是 坐 在 这 个 座 位 上, 可 是 那 时
船 在 江 心, 你 的 宝 剑 掉 在 江 心
了! 现 在 船 已 经 到 了 岸, 离 江 心
那 么 远, 你 再 从 这 个 地 方 跳 下
去, 怎 么 能 找 到 你 的 宝 剑 呢?"这
个 人 听 了, 才 知 道 自 己 做 错 了。

10. AN OLD MAN ON THE FRONTIER LOSES HIS HORSE

塞 翁 失 马

从 前, 有 一 个 老 人 和 他 的 儿 子

住在边境上，人们都叫他"塞翁"。塞翁跟村子里的人一样，养了很多马。每天早上，他和儿子都把马带到很远的地方去吃草，晚上再把它们带回家来。

有一天，塞翁的一匹马不见了。他找啊找啊，找了好几天，可是找不到。村里的人知道了，都觉得很可惜，大家都来安慰他。可是他们到他家的时候，看到他一点也不伤心。大家问他为什么不伤心。他说："马丢了我当然不高兴。不过丢了就丢了吧，我觉得不要太伤心，谁知道以后会怎么样呢？"

几个月过去了，塞翁丢的那匹马自己回来了，而且还带回来几匹高大漂亮的野马。村里的人为他高兴，都到他家来庆祝。

可是他们到他家的时候，却看到他并不特别高兴。大家问他为什么，他说："马回来了，而且还带回几匹野马，我当然高兴。可是野马不驯服就卖不出去，要驯服它们又很不容易。谁知道它们会不会给我家带来什么坏事呢？"

塞翁说得很对，这些野马真的很不容易驯服，驯服它们的时候，塞翁的儿子从马背上掉下来，受伤了，成了一个残疾人。村子里的人听说塞翁的儿子受伤了，都来安慰他。可是塞翁并不特别伤心，他对大家说："我的儿子虽然受伤了，成了残疾人，但是谁知道这不是一件好事呢？"

不久，边境上发生了战争，健康的男人都要去打仗。塞翁的儿子因为是个残疾人，不能去，只好留在家里。打仗的时候很多健康的男人都死了，而塞翁的儿子却因为是个残疾人，活下来了。

11. ONE OUT OF EVERY THREE MUST BE MY MENTOR

sān rén xíng bì yǒu wǒ shī
三 人 行 必 有 我 师

孔子是中国有名的思想家，他一共教过三千多个学生。他常常说："三人行，必有我师。"他觉得每三个人中，就有一个人可以做他的老师，因为每个人都有长处让他学习。

有一天，孔子和他的学生见到了一个国王。国王说："孔子，你是有名的大师，你能用线穿过这

个 珠 子 吗？"
gè zhū zi ma?

孔 子 把 珠 子 拿 过 来 看 了 看, 看
kǒng zǐ bǎ zhū zi ná guò lai kàn le kàn, kàn

见 珠 子 中 间 有 一 个 小 孔, 小 孔
jiàn zhū zi zhōng jiān yǒu yī gè xiǎo kǒng, xiǎo kǒng

又 小 又 弯 弯 曲 曲。他 和 他 的 学
yòu xiǎo yòu wān wān qū qū. tā hé tā de xué

生 想 了 很 多 办 法, 都 没 把 线 穿
shēng xiǎng le hěn duō bàn fǎ, dōu méi bǎ xiàn chuān

过 去。
guò qu.

这 时 候, 有 一 个 小 女 孩 从 旁 边
zhè shí hòu, yǒu yī gè xiǎo nǚ hái cóng páng biān

走 过。她 看 见 孔 子 穿 不 过 去, 就
zǒu guò. tā kàn jiàn kǒng zǐ chuān bú guò qu, jiù

对 他 说："这 很 容 易。你 把 线 拴 在
duì tā shuō: "zhè hěn róng yì. nǐ bǎ xiàn shuān zài

一 只 蚂 蚁 上, 让 蚂 蚁 从 珠 子 的
yī zhī mǎ yǐ shàng, ràng mǎ yǐ cóng zhū zi de

孔 里 爬 过 去, 线 就 能 穿 过 去 了。"
kǒng lǐ pá guò qu, xiàn jiù néng chuān guò qu le."

孔 子 听 了, 赶 快 找 了 一 只 蚂 蚁,
kǒng zǐ tīng le, gǎn kuài zhǎo le yī zhī mǎ yǐ,

很 快 就 把 线 穿 过 去 了。
hěn kuài jiù bǎ xiàn chuān guò qu le.

这 件 事 让 孔 子 想 了 很 久。他 对
zhè jiàn shì ràng kǒng zǐ xiǎng le hěn jiǔ. tā duì

学 生 说："你 看, 一 个 小 女 孩 子 也
xué shēng shuō: "nǐ kàn, yī gè xiǎo nǚ hái zi yě

可 以 教 我 们, 当 我 们 的 老 师。我
kě yǐ jiāo wǒ men, dāng wǒ men de lǎo shī. wǒ

们 真 应 该 好 好 向 每 个 人 学 习
men zhēn yīng gāi hǎo hǎo xiàng měi gè rén xué xí

啊。"
a.

mèng　mǔ　sān　qiān
孟　　母　　三　　迁

---

mèng	zǐ	shì	kǒng	zǐ	de	xué	shēng	yě	shì	hěn	yǒu
孟	子	是	孔	子	的	学	生，	也	是	很	有
míng	de	sī	xiǎng	jiā							
名	的	思	想	家。							

mèng	zǐ	xiǎo	de	shí	hòu	tā	jiā	lǐ	hěn	qióng	tā
孟	子	小	的	时	候，	他	家	里	很	穷。	他
de	fù	qīn	sǐ	de	hěn	zǎo	mǔ	qīn	fǔ	yǎng	tā
的	父	亲	死	得	很	早，	母	亲	抚	养	他。

mèng	zǐ	xiǎo	shí	hòu	bù	xǐ	huān	xué	xí	zhǐ	xiǎng
孟	子	小	时	候	不	喜	欢	学	习，	只	想
wánr		tā	de	mǔ	qīn	xiǎng	le	hěn	duō	bàn	fǎ
玩	儿，	他	的	母	亲	想	了	很	多	办	法
lái	bāng	zhù	tā	kāi	shǐ	tā	men	zhù	zài	yī	gè
来	帮	助	他。	开	始	他	们	住	在	一	个
mù	dì	páng	biān	xiǎo	mèng	zǐ	hé	bié	de	hái	zi
墓	地	旁	边，	小	孟	子	和	别	的	孩	子
yī	qǐ	xué	zhe	dà	rén	kū	wán	sǐ	rén	de	shìr
一	起，	学	着	大	人	哭，	玩	死	人	的	事
	mèng	zǐ	mā	ma	kàn	le	hěn	shēng	qì	tā	shuō
儿。	孟	子	妈	妈	看	了	很	生	气，	她	说：
zhè	bù	xíng	wǒ	bù	néng	ràng	wǒ	de	hái	zi	wán
"这	不	行，	我	不	能	让	我	的	孩	子	玩
zhè	gè	wǒ	men	bù	néng	zhù	zài	zhè	lǐ		
这	个，	我	们	不	能	住	在	这	里。"		

mèng	zǐ	hé	tā	mā	ma	bān	jiā	le	tā	men	bān
孟	子	和	他	妈	妈	搬	家	了。	他	们	搬
dào	yī	gè	jí	shì	páng	biān	mèng	zǐ	yòu	hé	bié
到	一	个	集	市	旁	边。	孟	子	又	和	别
de	hái	zi	yī	qǐ	xué	zhe	dà	rén	mǎi	mài	dōng
的	孩	子	一	起，	学	着	大	人	买	卖	东

西。孟子的妈妈又说："不行,这里
也不行,不适合我的孩子住。"

他们又搬家了。这一次他们搬
到了一个学校旁边。小孟子和
别的孩子一起,跟着老师学习,
慢慢儿喜欢念书了。孟子的妈
妈看了很高兴,说:"这才是适合
我儿子住的地方。"

因为孟子的母亲非常注意让
孟子从小就接受好的教育,所
以孟子长大以后成了有名的
思想家。

这就是孟母三迁的故事。后来
人们就用这个故事来说明只
有接近好的环境,才能养成好
的习惯,成为有用的人。

kǒng róng ràng lí
孔　融　让　梨

---

kǒng róng shì kǒng zǐ de dì èr shí dài zǐ sūn,
孔　融　是　孔　子　的　第　二　十　代　子　孙,

tā gēn kǒng zǐ yī yàng yě shì zhōng guó yǒu míng
他　跟　孔　子　一　样　也　是　中　国　有　名

de sī xiǎng jiā。 kǒng róng cóng xiǎo jiù shì gè hǎo
的　思　想　家。　孔　融　从　小　就　是　个　好

hái zi。
孩　子。

kǒng róng chū shēng zài yī gè dà jiā tíng lǐ。 tā
孔　融　出　生　在　一　个　大　家　庭　里。　他

yǒu wǔ gè gē gē, yī gè dì dì。 kǒng róng sì
有　五　个　哥　哥,　一　个　弟　弟。　孔　融　四

suì de shí hòu, yǒu yī tiān, bà ba gěi hái zi
岁　的　时　候,　有　一　天,　爸　爸　给　孩　子

men chī lí, tā ràng kǒng róng xiān ná。 kǒng róng kàn
们　吃　梨,　他　让　孔　融　先　拿。　孔　融　看

le kàn pán zi lǐ de lí, shēn chū shǒu qù, ná
了　看　盘　子　里　的　梨,　伸　出　手　去,　拿

le yī gè zuì xiǎo zuì bù hǎo de。
了　一　个　最　小　最　不　好　的。

bà ba kàn le, jué de hěn qí guài, jiù wèn kǒng
爸　爸　看　了,　觉　得　很　奇　怪,　就　问　孔

róng: "zhè me duō de lí, wǒ ràng nǐ xiān ná, nǐ
融:　"这　么　多　的　梨,　我　让　你　先　拿,　你

wèi shén me zhǐ ná le yī gè zuì xiǎo de ne?"
为　什　么　只　拿　了　一　个　最　小　的　呢?"

kǒng róng xiào zhe shuō: "wǒ nián jì xiǎo, yīng gāi chī
孔　融　笑　着　说:　"我　年　纪　小,　应　该　吃

xiǎo	de	dà	de	liú	gěi	gē	gē	men	chī	ba	
小	的;	大	的	留	给	哥	哥	们	吃	吧。	"

bà	ba	yòu	wèn	nà	dì	dì	ne	tā	de	nián	jì
爸	爸	又	问:	"那	弟	弟	呢,	他	的	年	纪

bú	shì	gèng	xiǎo	ma
不	是	更	小	吗? "

kǒng	róng	yòu	shuō	wǒ	bǐ	dì	dì	dà	suǒ	yǐ	yīng
孔	融	又	说:	"我	比	弟	弟	大,	所	以	应

gāi	bǎ	dà	de	lí	liú	gěi	dì	dì	chī
该	把	大	的	梨	留	给	弟	弟	吃。 "

bà	ba	tīng	le	hěn	gāo	xìng	shuō	kǒng	róng	zhēn	shì
爸	爸	听	了,	很	高	兴,	说:	"孔	融	真	是

yī	gè	hǎo	hái	zi
一	个	好	孩	子。 "

dà	jiā	dōu	kuā	kǒng	róng	shì	gè	yǒu	ài	xīn	de
大	家	都	夸	孔	融	是	个	有	爱	心	的

hǎo	hái	zi	shuō	tā	zhēn	shì	kǒng	zǐ	de	hǎo	zǐ
好	孩	子,	说	他	真	是	孔	子	的	好	子

sūn
孙。

14. GRINDING DOWN AN IRON PESTLE TO A NEEDLE

tiě	chǔ	mó	chéng	zhēn
铁	杵	磨	成	针

---

dà	shī	rén	lǐ	bái	xiě	le	hěn	duō	yōu	měi	de
大	诗	人	李	白	写	了	很	多	优	美	的

shī	zhí	dào	jīn	tiān	rén	men	hái	shì	hěn	xǐ	huān
诗。	直	到	今	天,	人	们	还	是	很	喜	欢

dú	tā	de	shī	shuō	tā	de	gù	shì	tiě	chǔ	mó
读	他	的	诗,	说	他	的	故	事。	铁	杵	磨

chéng	zhēn	shì	tā	xiǎo	shí	hòu	de	gù	shì
成	针	是	他	小	时	候	的	故	事。

李白小的时候一点也不喜欢念书，常常逃学，到学校外面去玩。

有一天，老师让他念书，他念到一半，又跑出去玩了。

这天很热，小李白就跑到河边去玩。他看见一位老奶奶拿着一根大铁杵在一块大石头上磨呀磨呀。老奶奶磨得很认真，满头都是汗。

小李白觉得很奇怪，就问："你在做什么呀，老奶奶？"

老奶奶一边磨着，一边说："我在磨这根铁杵呀。"

小李白觉得更奇怪了，又问："磨这个做什么么啊？"

老奶奶抬起头，看了看李白说，

<pre>
zuò   yī   gēn   zhēn   yā
"做   一   根   针   呀。"

shén   me   xiǎo   lǐ   bái   dà   jiào   qǐ   lai   nǐ   xiǎng bǎ
"什   么?!"   小   李   白   大   叫   起   来，"你   想   把

zhè   me   cū   de   tiě   chǔ   mó   chéng xiǎo   xiǎo   de   zhēn
这   么   粗   的   铁   杵   磨   成   小   小   的   针?!

zhè   kě   shì   yào   duō   shào   nián   de   shí   jiān   yā
这   可   是   要   多   少   年   的   时   间   呀！"

nǐ   shuō   de   hěn   duì   zhè   shì   yào   hěn   cháng de   shí
"你   说   得   很   对，   这   是   要   很   长   的   时

jiān   kě   shì   zhǐ   yào   wǒ   yī   zhí   mó   xià   qù   wǒ
间。   可   是，   只   要   我   一   直   磨   下   去，   我

yī   dìng   néng   bǎ   tā   mó   chéng zhēn   de
一   定   能   把   它   磨   成   针   的。"

lǎo   rén   de   huà   shēn   shēn   de   dǎ   dòng   le   xiǎo   lǐ
老   人   的   话   深   深   地   打   动   了   小   李

bái   cóng   cǐ   tā   rèn   zhēn   xué   xí   chéng le   yī   wèi
白，   从   此，   他   认   真   学   习，   成   了   一   位

dà   shī   rén
大   诗   人。

hòu   lái   rén   men   cháng cháng bǎ   tiě   chǔ   mó   chéng zhēn
后   来，   人   们   常   常   把   "铁   杵   磨   成   针"

yòng   lái   shuō   míng   yī   gè   rén   zhǐ   yào   yǒu   rèn   zhēn
用   来   说   明   一   个   人   只   要   有   认   真，

jiù   yī   dìng   néng   gòu   chéng gōng   zuò   dào   tā   xiǎng yào
就   一   定   能   够   成   功，   做   到   他   想   要

zuò   de   shì   qíng
做   的   事   情。
</pre>

fù	jīng	qǐng	zuì
负	荆	请	罪

---

lián 廉	pō 颇	shì 是	zhào 赵	guó 国	de 的	dà 大	jiàng 将	jūn 军。	tā 他	dǎ 打	guò 过
hěn 很	duō 多	shèng 胜	zhàng 仗,	lì 立	guò 过	hěn 很	duō 多	gōng 功	láo 劳。	zhào 赵	guó 国
de 的	guó 国	wáng 王	hěn 很	xǐ 喜	huān 欢	tā 他,	suǒ 所	yǐ 以	lián 廉	pō 颇	hěn 很
jiāo 骄	ào 傲。	hòu 后	lái 来,	yī 一	wèi 位	jiào 叫	lìn 蔺	xiāng 相	rú 如	de 的	rén 人
yě 也	bāng 帮	zhào 赵	guó 国	zuò 作	le 了	hěn 很	duō 多	dà 大	shì 事,	lì 立	le 了
hěn 很	duō 多	gōng 功	láo 劳,	zhào 赵	wáng 王	yě 也	hěn 很	xǐ 喜	huān 欢	tā 他,	ràng 让
tā 他	zuò 作	le 了	guān 官,	guān 官	bǐ 比	lián 廉	pō 颇	jiāng 将	jūn 军	hái 还	dà 大。

lián 廉	pō 颇	hěn 很	bù 不	gāo 高	xìng 兴,	tā 他	shuō 说:"	wǒ 我	shì 是	zhào 赵	guó 国
de 的	dà 大	jiàng 将	jūn 军,	dǎ 打	le 了	hěn 很	duō 多	shèng 胜	zhàng 仗,	lì 立	le 了
hěn 很	duō 多	gōng 功	láo 劳。	lìn 蔺	xiāng 相	rú 如	de 的	guān 官	hái 还	bǐ 比	wǒ 我
de 的	dà 大。	hēng 哼!	wǒ 我	yào 要	shì 是	jiàn 见	dào 到	lìn 蔺	xiāng 相	rú 如,	jiù 就
yào 要	duì 对	tā 他	bù 不	kè 客	qì 气!"						

| lián 廉 | pō 颇 | de 的 | huà 话 | lìn 蔺 | xiāng 相 | rú 如 | tīng 听 | dào 到 | le 了, | tā 他 | jiù 就 |
| hěn 很 | xiǎo 小 | xīn 心, | dào 到 | chù 处 | duǒ 躲 | zhe 着 | lián 廉 | pō 颇。 | | | |

| yǒu 有 | yī 一 | tiān 天, | lìn 蔺 | xiāng 相 | rú 如 | kàn 看 | jiàn 见 | lián 廉 | pō 颇 | lái 来 | le 了, |

jiù dào páng biān qù duǒ yī duǒ, ràng lián pō xiān
就 到 旁 边 去 躲 一 躲, 让 廉 颇 先
zǒu
走。

lìn xiāng rú de pú rén hěn shēng qì, tā men dōu
蔺 相 如 的 仆 人 很 生 气, 他 们 都
shuō lìn xiāng rú bù yīng gāi zhè me pà lián pō。
说 蔺 相 如 不 应 该 这 么 怕 廉 颇。

lìn xiāng rú tīng le, xiào zhe wèn tā men: "nǐ men
蔺 相 如 听 了, 笑 着 问 他 们: "你 们
kàn lián pō jiāng jūn hé qín guó de guó wáng nǎ
看 廉 颇 将 军 和 秦 国 的 国 王, 哪
yī gè gèng kě pà?"
一 个 更 可 怕?"

pú rén men shuō: "nà dāng rán shì qín guó de guó
仆 人 们 说: "那 当 然 是 秦 国 的 国
wáng gèng kě pà le。"
王 更 可 怕 了。"

lìn xiāng rú shuō: "duì yā! qín guó de guó wáng nà
蔺 相 如 说: "对 呀! 秦 国 的 国 王 那
me kě pà, rén rén dōu pà tā, kě shì wǒ bù
么 可 怕, 人 人 都 怕 他, 可 是 我 不
pà。 nà wèi shén me wǒ pà lián pō jiāng jūn ne?
怕。 那 为 什 么 我 怕 廉 颇 将 军 呢?
yīn wèi qín guó bù lái jìn gōng zhào guó, jiù shì
因 为 秦 国 不 来 进 攻 赵 国, 就 是
yīn wèi yǒu wǒ hé lián pō jiāng jūn。 yào shì wǒ
因 为 有 我 和 廉 颇 将 军。 要 是 我
men liǎng gè rén bù hé, qín guó jiù huì lái jìn
们 两 个 人 不 和, 秦 国 就 会 来 进
gōng。 wǒ duǒ zhe lián pō jiāng jūn, bú shì pà tā,
攻。 我 躲 着 廉 颇 将 军, 不 是 怕 他,
ér shì wèi le wǒ men de guó jiā a。"
而 是 为 了 我 们 的 国 家 啊。"

hòu lái, yǒu rén gào su le lián pō zhè xiē huà.
后来，有人告诉了廉颇这些话。

lián pō tīng le yǐ hòu, xiǎng le hěn jiǔ, zhī dào
廉颇听了以后，想了很久，知道

zì jǐ cuò le. tā jiù bèi zhe yī gēn hěn cū
自己错了。他就背着一根很粗

de jīng tiáo, dào lìn xiāng rú jiā lǐ qù qǐng zuì.
的荆条，到蔺相如家里去请罪。

lián pō jiàn le lìn xiāng rú jiù shuō: "wǒ cuò le,
廉颇见了蔺相如就说："我错了，

wǒ tài jiāo ào le. nín wèi le guó jiā, duì wǒ
我太骄傲了。您为了国家，对我

zhè me hǎo. qǐng nín yòng zhè gēn jīng tiáo dǎ wǒ
这么好。请您用这根荆条打我

ba."
吧。"

lìn xiāng rú gǎn kuài bǎ jīng tiáo cóng lián pō bèi
蔺相如赶快把荆条从廉颇背

shàng ná xià lai, shuō: "lián pō jiāng jūn bú yào zhè
上拿下来，说："廉颇将军不要这

yàng. wǒ men liǎng gè rén dōu shì zhào guó de dà
样。我们两个人都是赵国的大

jiàng jūn, yīng gāi yī qǐ wèi guó jiā fú wù. nín
将军，应该一起为国家服务。您

néng gòu lǐ jiě wǒ, wǒ yǐ jīng hěn gāo xìng le,
能够理解我，我已经很高兴了，

zěn me hái néng ràng nín lái gěi wǒ dào qiàn ne."
怎么还能让您来给我道歉呢。"

jiù zhè yàng, tā men chéng le zuì hǎo de péng you,
就这样，他们成了最好的朋友，

yī qǐ wèi zhào guó lì le hěn duō gōng láo.
一起为赵国立了很多功劳。

"fù jīng qǐng zuì" jiù shì shuō, zhī dào zì jǐ cuò
"负荆请罪"就是说，知道自己错

le, jiù qù xiàng bié rén dào qiàn.
了，就去向别人道歉。

cáo chōng chēng xiàng
曹 冲 称 象

---

cáo chōng shì cáo cāo de zuì xiǎo de ér zi tā
曹 冲 是 曹 操 的 最 小 的 儿 子，他
cóng xiǎo jiù hěn cōng míng
从 小 就 很 聪 明。

yǒu yī cì yǒu rén sòng gěi cáo cāo yī zhī dà
有 一 次，有 人 送 给 曹 操 一 只 大
xiàng cáo cāo hěn gāo xìng jiù wèn tā de guān yuán
象。曹 操 很 高 兴，就 问 他 的 官 员：
nǐ men shéi zhī dào zhè zhī dà xiàng yǒu duō zhòng
"你 们 谁 知 道 这 只 大 象 有 多 重
ma tā men hù xiāng kàn le kàn shéi yě bù zhī
吗？"他 们 互 相 看 了 看，谁 也 不 知
dào tā yǒu duō zhòng
道 她 有 多 重。

cáo cāo yòu wèn tā men nǐ men shéi yǒu bàn fǎ
曹 操 又 问 他 们："你 们 谁 有 办 法
bǎ dà xiàng chēng yī chēng zhè kě shì tài nán le
把 大 象 称 一 称？"这 可 是 太 难 了。
dà xiàng shì zuì dà de dòng wù nà shí hòu méi
大 象 是 最 大 的 动 物。那 时 候 没
yǒu nà me dà de chèng zěn me chēng ne guān yuán
有 那 么 大 的 秤，怎 么 称 呢？官 员
men wéi zhe dà xiàng kàn lai kàn qu dōu bù zhī
们 围 着 大 象 看 来 看 去，都 不 知
dào zěn me bàn
道 怎 么 办。

zhè shí hòu yī gè xiǎo hái zi pǎo chū lai duì
这 时 候，一 个 小 孩 子 跑 出 来，对
dà jiā shuō wǒ yǒu bàn fǎ wǒ yǒu bàn fǎ dà
大 家 说："我 有 办 法，我 有 办 法!"大

家 一 看，是 曹 操 的 小 儿 子 曹 冲，
心 里 就 想："大 人 都 想 不 出 办 法
来，一 个 五 岁 的 小 孩 子，会 有 什
么 办 法？"

他 爸 爸 笑 着 说："好！你 有 办 法，快
说 出 来 给 大 家 听 听。"曹 冲 说："我
称 给 你 们 看，你 们 就 知 道 了。"

小 曹 冲 叫 人 牵 着 大 象，跟 他 一
起 到 河 边 去。他 的 爸 爸，还 有 那
些 官 员 们 都 想 看 看 他 怎 么 称
大 象，就 也 去 了 河 边。

河 里 有 一 只 大 船，曹 冲 说："把 大
象 牵 到 船 上 去。"大 象 上 了 船，船
就 往 下 沉 了 一 些。曹 冲 说："齐 着
水 面 在 船 边 上 做 一 个 记 号。"

记 号 做 好 了 以 后，曹 冲 又 叫 人
把 大 象 牵 上 岸 来。这 时 候 大 船
空 着，大 船 就 往 上 浮 起 一 些 来。

大家看着，一会儿把大象牵上船，一会儿又把大象牵下船，心里都说:"这孩子在做什么呀?"

然后，小曹冲又叫人拿了很多石头，放到船里去，大船又开始慢慢地往下沉了。

"好了，好了!"曹冲看见船边上的记号齐水面了，就叫人把石头拿下船来，放在秤上称。

大家还是不知道曹冲在做什么，小曹冲笑着说:"石头和大象放进船里以后，船边上的记号都齐水面了，那么，石头和大象就是一样重了。如果我们把这些石头都称一称，不就是大象的重量了吗?"

大家听了，都夸曹冲，说:"这办法听起来虽然简单，可是大人还

méi xiǎng dào ne. tā nián jì zhè me xiǎo, jiù zhī
没　想　到　呢。他　年　纪　这　么　小，就　知
dào zěn yàng chēng dà xiàng zhēn shì gè cōng míng de
道　怎　样　称　大　象。真　是　个　聪　明　的
hǎo hái zi!"
好　孩　子！"

17. BREAKING THE WATER VAT TO SAVE A LIFE

sī mǎ guāng zá gāng
司　马　光　砸　缸

sī mǎ guāng hěn xiǎo de shí hòu jiù hěn xǐ huān
司　马　光　很　小　的　时　候　就　很　喜　欢
xué xí. tā cháng cháng zhuān xīn dú shū, yǒu shí hòu
学　习。他　常　常　专　心　读　书，有　时　候
lián chī fàn hē shuǐ dōu wàng jì le. sī mǎ guāng
连　吃　饭　喝　水　都　忘　记　了。司　马　光
bú dàn hěn xǐ huān xué xí, ér qiě hái hěn cōng
不　但　很　喜　欢　学　习，而　且　还　很　聪
míng, yǒng gǎn. yǒu yī gè gù shì tè bié yǒu míng,
明，勇　敢。有　一　个　故　事　特　别　有　名，
dào jīn tiān rén men dōu hái jì de.
到　今　天　人　们　都　还　记　得。

sī mǎ guāng qī suì de shí hòu, yǒu yī cì tā
司　马　光　七　岁　的　时　候，有　一　次，他
gēn xiǎo péng you men zài jiā lǐ zhuō mí cáng. tā
跟　小　朋　友　们　在　家　里　捉　迷　藏。他
jiā lǐ fàng zhe yī kǒu dà shuǐ gāng, shuǐ gāng lǐ
家　里　放　着　一　口　大　水　缸，水　缸　里
zhuāng mǎn le shuǐ.
装　满　了　水。

yǒu yī gè xiǎo péng you kuài yào bèi zhuō zhù le,
有　一　个　小　朋　友　快　要　被　捉　住　了，
jiù gǎn kuài pá dào shuǐ gāng shàng mian qù. kě shì,
就　赶　快　爬　到　水　缸　上　面　去。可　是，

212　　　　　*Appendix: Simplified Characters with* Pinyin

yī bù xiǎo xīn, tā diào dào shuǐ gāng lǐ qù le.
一 不 小 心, 他 掉 到 水 缸 里 去 了。

shuǐ gāng hěn dà, shuǐ hěn shēn, nà hái zi zài lǐ miàn yòu hǎn yòu jiào, jiù yào chén xià qù le. bié de hái zi kàn dào le, pà jí le, yī qǐ dà kū qǐ lai. yǒu de wǎng wài miàn pǎo, qù zhǎo bà ba mā ma lái bāng máng.
水 缸 很 大, 水 很 深, 那 孩 子 在 里 面 又 喊 又 叫, 就 要 沉 下 去 了。别 的 孩 子 看 到 了, 怕 极 了, 一 起 大 哭 起 来。有 的 往 外 面 跑, 去 找 爸 爸 妈 妈 来 帮 忙。

xiǎo sī mǎ guāng kàn dào shuǐ gāng lǐ de hái zi kuài yào chén xià qù le, rú guǒ děng dà rén lái jiù, jiù huì tài wǎn le. tā xiǎng le xiǎng, jiù cóng dì shang zhǎo lái yī kuài dà shí tóu, wǎng shuǐ gāng shàng mian zá le guò qu.
小 司 马 光 看 到 水 缸 里 的 孩 子 快 要 沉 下 去 了, 如 果 等 大 人 来 救, 就 会 太 晚 了。他 想 了 想, 就 从 地 上 找 来 一 块 大 石 头, 往 水 缸 上 面 砸 了 过 去。

zhǐ tīng jiàn "pēng" de yī shēng, shuǐ gāng bèi zá pò le, gāng lǐ de shuǐ hěn kuài liú le chū lai, gāng lǐ de xiǎo hái yě jiù jiù chū lai le.
只 听 见 "砰" 的 一 声, 水 缸 被 砸 破 了, 缸 里 的 水 很 快 流 了 出 来, 缸 里 的 小 孩 也 就 救 出 来 了。

xiǎo hái de bà ba mā ma zhī dào le zhè jiàn shì qíng, fēi cháng gǎn jī sī mǎ guāng, duì tā shuō: "nǐ zhēn shì gè cōng míng yǒng gǎn de hǎo hái zi, jiù le wǒ men de ér zi."
小 孩 的 爸 爸 妈 妈 知 道 了 这 件 事 情, 非 常 感 激 司 马 光, 对 他 说:"你 真 是 个 聪 明 勇 敢 的 好 孩 子, 救 了 我 们 的 儿 子。"

zhí　dào　jīn　tiān,　dà　jiā　hái　hěn　pèi　fú　tā,　shuō
直　到　今　天,　大　家　还　很　佩　服　他,　说

tā　zhè　me　xiǎo　xiǎo　de　nián　jì　jiù　zhè　me　cōng
他　这　么　小　小　的　年　纪　就　这　么　聪

míng　yǒng　gǎn
明　勇　敢。

18. BIRD JINGWEI FILLS UP THE SEA

jīng　wèi　tián　hǎi
精　卫　填　海

---

chuán　shuō　hěn　jiǔ　yǐ　qián,　yǒu　yī　gè　yán　dì,　tā
传　说　很　久　以　前,　有　一　个　炎　帝,　他

yǒu　yī　gè　yòu　cōng　míng　yòu　kě　ài　de　nǚ　ér,
有　一　个　又　聪　明　又　可　爱　的　女　儿,

jiào　nǚ　wá.　yán　dì　hěn　ài　tā　de　nǚ　ér,　kě
叫　女　娃。　炎　帝　很　爱　他　的　女　儿,　可

shì　tā　tiān　tiān　hěn　máng,　méi　yǒu　shí　jiān　gēn　tā
是　他　天　天　很　忙,　没　有　时　间　跟　她

yī　qǐ　wánr　　nǚ　wá　jiù　cháng　cháng　zì　jǐ　yī
一　起　玩　儿。　女　娃　就　常　常　自　己　一

gè　rén　zuò　zhe　xiǎo　chuán,　dào　gè　dì　qù　wánr　儿。
个　人　坐　着　小　船,　到　各　地　去　玩　儿。

tā　qù　le　hěn　duō　yǒu　yì　sī　de　dì　fāng.　yǒu
她　去　了　很　多　有　意　思　的　地　方。　有

yī　tiān,　tā　xiǎng　dào　hěn　yuǎn　de　dì　fāng　qù　kàn
一　天,　她　想　到　很　远　的　地　方　去　看

kàn.　kě　shì,　zhè　yī　tiān　hǎi　shàng　guā　qǐ　le　dà
看。　可　是,　这　一　天　海　上　刮　起　了　大

fēng,　xià　qǐ　le　dà　yǔ,　hǎi　làng　xiàng　xiǎo　shān　yī
风,　下　起　了　大　雨,　海　浪　像　小　山　一

yàng,　bǎ　tā　de　chuán　dǎ　fān　le.　jiù　zhè　yàng,　nǚ
样,　把　她　的　船　打　翻　了。　就　这　样,　女

wá　bèi　dà　hǎi　yān　sǐ　le,　zài　yě　huí　bù　lai
娃　被　大　海　淹　死　了,　再　也　回　不　来

了。炎帝很伤心，常常哭着，叫着
女儿的名字。

女娃虽然淹死了，可是她的灵
魂变成了一只可爱的小鸟。它
一边飞，一边叫着，"精卫、精卫，"所
以，人们都把它叫做"精卫。"

精卫仇恨大海，因为它淹死了
自己，从此不能跟爸爸妈妈在
一起了，让爸爸妈妈很伤心。她
要报仇，要把大海填平！因此，她
找来一粒粒小石头，和一根根
小树枝，一直飞到大海，把石子
和树枝投下去。她天天这样，飞
个不停，一定要把大海填平。

大海笑她，说："小鸟，你那么小，每
天投下这么一点点，你投一万
年，也不能把我填平啊。"

精卫回答说："一万年，就是一百

wàn nián, wǒ yě yī dìng yào bǎ nǐ tián píng!"
万　年，我　也　一　定　要　把　你　填　平！"

dà hǎi yòu wèn: "nà nǐ wèi shén me yī dìng yào
大　海　又　问："那　你　为　什　么　一　定　要

bǎ wǒ tián píng ne?"
把　我　填　平　呢？"

jīng wèi shuō: "yīn wèi nǐ yān sǐ le wǒ, nǐ yǐ
精　卫　说："因　为　你　淹　死　了　我，你　以

hòu hái huì yān sǐ hěn duō bié de rén, suǒ yǐ
后　还　会　淹　死　很　多　别　的　人，所　以

wǒ yī dìng yào bǎ nǐ tián píng!"
我　一　定　要　把　你　填　平！"

rén men dōu hěn pèi fú jīng wèi, jué de tā yòu
人　们　都　很　佩　服　精　卫，觉　得　她　又

jiān qiáng yòu yǒu yì lì, yī dìng néng chéng gōng.
坚　强　又　有　毅　力，一　定　能　成　功。

19. GODDESS NUWA MENDS THE SKY

nǚ wā bǔ tiān
女　娲　补　天

---

chuán shuō hěn jiǔ hěn jiǔ yǐ qián zhōng guó yǒu yī
传　说　很　久　很　久　以　前　中　国　有　一

wèi měi lì de nǚ shén, tā de míng zì jiào nǚ
位　美　丽　的　女　神，她　的　名　字　叫　女

wā. nǚ wā shì yī wèi hěn shàn liáng de shén, tā
娲。女　娲　是　一　位　很　善　良　的　神，她

wèi rén men zuò le hěn duō hǎo shì. tā chuàng zào
为　人　们　做　了　很　多　好　事。她　创　造

le rén, yòu jiào tā men jié hūn shēng hái zi.
了　人，又　教　他　们　结　婚　生　孩　子。

kě shì, zuì ràng rén men gǎn dòng de, shì tā bǔ
可　是，最　让　人　们　感　动　的，是　她　补

tiān de gù shì.
天　的　故　事。

yǒu yī tiān, shuǐ shén hé huǒ shén dǎ qǐ lai le.
有 一 天，水 神 和 火 神 打 起 来 了。

tā men cóng tiān shàng yī zhí dǎ dào dì xià, bǎ
他 们 从 天 上 一 直 打 到 地 下，把

tiān dǎ pò le, shàng mian chū le yī gè hěn dà
天 打 破 了，上 面 出 了 一 个 很 大

de dòng. tiān pò le yǐ hòu, tā hěn kuài jiù tā
的 洞。天 破 了 以 后，它 很 快 就 塌

xià lai le, dì yě liè kāi le, dào chù dōu shì
下 来 了，地 也 裂 开 了，到 处 都 是

dà huǒ, shuǐ yě cóng dì xià pēn chū lai le. hěn
大 火，水 也 从 地 下 喷 出 来 了。很

duō rén dōu bìng le, sǐ le.
多 人 都 病 了，死 了。

nǚ wā kàn jiàn le, xīn lǐ hěn zháo jí, yě hěn
女 娲 看 见 了，心 里 很 着 急，也 很

shāng xīn. tā yī dìng yào wèi rén men zài zuò yī
伤 心。她 一 定 要 为 人 们 再 做 一

jiàn dà shì, nà jiù shì bǎ tā xià lai de tiān
件 大 事，那 就 是 把 它 塌 下 来 的 天

bǔ hǎo! nǚ wā zhǎo lái le gè zhǒng yán sè de
补 好！女 娲 找 来 了 各 种 颜 色 的

shí tou, yòng huǒ bǎ tā men biàn chéng le shí jiāng,
石 头，用 火 把 它 们 变 成 了 石 浆，

zài yòng zhè zhòng shí jiāng bǎ tiān shàng de dòng bǔ
再 用 这 种 石 浆 把 天 上 的 洞 补

hǎo. rán hòu, nǚ wā zài yòng dà guī de jiǎo, bǎ
好。然 后，女 娲 再 用 大 龟 的 脚，把

tā xià lai de tiān zhī chēng qǐ lai le.
它 塌 下 来 的 天 支 撑 起 来 了。

nǚ wā jiù zhè yàng yī zhí máng zhe, tā xiān bǎ
女 娲 就 这 样 一 直 忙 着，她 先 把

tiān bǔ hǎo, zài bǎ dì tián píng le, rán hòu yòu
天 补 好，再 把 地 填 平 了，然 后 又

bǎ huǒ hé shuǐ dōu tíng le. rén men yòu kě yǐ
把 火 和 水 都 停 了。人 们 又 可 以

快乐地生活了。但是女娲累病了。人们都去看她，为她的病着急。可是，女娲笑着说:"我病了没关系，只要我能帮助大家，让你们过得快乐，我就高兴了。"

因此，人们都很感激女娲，希望她的病快点好起来，可是女娲还是病死了。她死了以后，人们常常想着她，感谢她为大家作了那么多好事情。在人们的心中，女娲永远是一位美丽善良的女神。

20. PANGU CREATES THE UNIVERSE

pán gǔ kāi tiān dì
盘 古 开 天 地

很久很久以前，天和地合在一起。宇宙就像一个大鸡蛋，里面黑黑的，没有上下左右，也没有

东 南 西 北。 可 是, 这 个 鸡 蛋 里 睡

着 一 个 大 英 雄, 他 就 是 盘 古。

盘 古 在 这 个 大 鸡 蛋 里 睡 了 一

万 八 千 年。 有 一 天, 他 醒 过 来 了,

往 四 面 看 看, 可 是 到 处 都 是 黑

黑 的, 什 么 也 看 不 见。 鸡 蛋 里 面

不 但 很 黑, 而 且 又 闷 又 热。 盘 古

想 站 起 来, 可 是 鸡 蛋 包 着 他 的

身 体, 他 一 下 都 不 能 动。

盘 古 觉 得 很 不 舒 服, 他 到 处 摸

摸, 找 到 了 一 把 大 斧 子。 他 用 力

挥 动 斧 子, 只 听 见 "砰" 的 一 声, 大

鸡 蛋 裂 开 了, 里 面 轻 的 东 西 往

上 升 变 成 了 天, 重 的 东 西, 往 下

掉, 变 成 了 地。 从 那 以 后, 宇 宙 就

不 再 是 一 个 大 鸡 蛋 了, 而 是 有

了 天 和 地。

盘 古 打 开 了 天 和 地, 他 高 兴 极

了。 他 的 头 顶 着 天， 脚 踩 着 地， 支
撑 着 天 和 地。 盘 古 又 高 又 大， 而
且 每 天 都 长 高 一 丈。 他 每 长 一
丈， 天 就 升 高 一 丈， 地 也 就 增 厚
一 丈。 就 这 样， 天 变 得 越 来 高 越
高， 地 也 变 得 越 来 越 厚。

盘 古 就 这 样 站 着， 过 了 一 万 八
千 年 以 后， 他 累 极 了， 所 以 躺 下
来， 闭 上 了 眼 睛， 可 是 他 就 再 也
醒 不 过 来 了。 盘 古 死 了 以 后， 他
的 身 体 变 成 了 高 山， 血 液 变 成
了 大 河， 毛 发 也 变 成 了 花 草 和
树 木。

人 们 感 激 盘 古 打 开 了 天 和 地，
又 把 自 己 的 身 体 变 成 了 美 丽
的 山 河。 所 以， 在 人 们 的 心 中， 他
永 远 是 一 个 大 英 雄。

21. DA YU CONTROLS THE GREAT FLOOD

dà　yǔ　zhì　shuǐ
大　禹　治　水

---

chuán shuō hěn duō hěn duō nián yǐ qián zhōng guó cháng
传　说　很　多　很　多　年　以　前，中　国　常

cháng fā shēng dà shuǐ fā dà shuǐ de shí hòu rén
常　发　生　大　水。发　大　水　的　时　候，人

men de fáng zi tā le tián bèi yān le hěn duō
们　的　房　子　塌　了，田　被　淹　了，很　多

rén yě dōu bèi yān sǐ le dà yǔ de fù qīn
人　也　都　被　淹　死　了。大　禹　的　父　亲

gēn rén men yī qǐ xiǎng bàn fǎ qù zhì zhè xiē
跟　人　们　一　起，想　办　法　去　治　这　些

dà shuǐ kě shì méi yǒu chéng gōng dà yǔ zhǎng dà
大　水，可　是　没　有　成　功。大　禹　长　大

le yǐ hòu jué de yī dìng yào xiàng fù qīn yī
了　以　后，觉　得　一　定　要　像　父　亲　一

yàng qù wèi dà jiā zhì shuǐ ràng rén men kuài lè
样，去　为　大　家　治　水，让　人　们　快　乐

de shēng huó
地　生　活。

dà yǔ shì yī gè yòu rèn zhēn yòu cōng míng de
大　禹　是　一　个　又　认　真　又　聪　明　的

rén tā zhì shuǐ yǐ qián xiān xiǎng xiǎng fù qīn yǐ
人。他　治　水　以　前，先　想　想　父　亲　以

qián shì zěn yàng zhì shuǐ de rán hòu jiù zì jǐ
前　是　怎　样　治　水　的，然　后　就　自　己

dào hěn duō dà hé qù kǎo chá kàn kàn nà lǐ
到　很　多　大　河　去　考　察　看　看　那　里

de qíng kuàng zài hé rén men yī qǐ tǎo lùn dà
的　情　况，再　和　人　们　一　起　讨　论。大

yǔ kǎo chá wán le yǐ hòu duì dà hé de qíng
禹　考　察　完　了　以　后，对　大　河　的　情

kuàng zuò le rèn zhēn yán jiū jiù dài zhe dà jiā
况　作　了　认　真　研　究，就　带　着　大　家

kāi shǐ zhì shuǐ le zhì shuǐ de rén gōng zuò de
开 始 治 水 了。 治 水 的 人 工 作 得

hěn rèn zhēn yě hěn xīn kǔ yǒu shí hòu lián fàn
很 认 真, 也 很 辛 苦, 有 时 候 连 饭

dōu chī bù bǎo kě hái shì yī zhí gōng zuò dào
都 吃 不 饱, 可 还 是 一 直 工 作 到

bàn yè dà yǔ de tuǐ dōu lèi zhǒng le dàn hái
半 夜。 大 禹 的 腿 都 累 肿 了, 但 还

shì bù tíng xià lai yī zhí nǔ lì de gōng zuò
是 不 停 下 来, 一 直 努 力 地 工 作。

jiù zhè yàng dà yǔ gēn rén men yī qǐ nǔ lì
就 这 样, 大 禹 跟 人 们 一 起 努 力

zhì shuǐ tā gōng zuò de tài rèn zhēn le hěn duō
治 水。 他 工 作 得 太 认 真 了, 很 多

nián dōu méi yǒu huí jiā yǒu hǎo jǐ cì tā lù
年 都 没 有 回 家。 有 好 几 次 他 路

guò zì jǐ jiā de mén kǒu dàn shì méi yǒu jìn
过 自 己 家 的 门 口, 但 是 没 有 进

qù
去。

dì yī cì dà yǔ lù guò jiā mén kǒu de shí
第 一 次 大 禹 路 过 家 门 口 的 时

hòu tā de qī zi yào shēng hái zi le rén men
候, 他 的 妻 子 要 生 孩 子 了, 人 们

dōu yào tā jìn qù kàn yī kàn kě shì dà yǔ
都 要 他 进 去 看 一 看, 可 是 大 禹

shuō zhì shuǐ hái méi yǒu chéng gōng wǒ zěn me néng
说:"治 水 还 没 有 成 功, 我 怎 么 能

huí jiā ne dì èr cì lù guò jiā mén kǒu de
回 家 呢?" 第 二 次 路 过 家 门 口 的

shí hòu dà yǔ pà yǐng xiǎng zhì shuǐ hái shì méi
时 候, 大 禹 怕 影 响 治 水, 还 是 没

yǒu jìn qù yòu yǒu yī cì dà yǔ de qī zi
有 进 去。 又 有 一 次, 大 禹 的 妻 子

zài jiā mén kǒu kàn jiàn le tā gāo xìng jí le
在 家 门 口 看 见 了 他, 高 兴 极 了,

yào tā huí jiā qù kàn kàn hái zi kě shì tā
要 他 回 家 去 看 看 孩 子, 可 是 他

hái	shì	méi	yǒu	jìn	qù。	jiù	zhè	yàng,	dà	yǔ	bǎ
还	是	没	有	进	去。	就	这	样，	大	禹	把
tā	de	shí	jiān	dōu	yòng	lái	zhì	shuǐ	le,	tā	de
他	的	时	间	都	用	来	治	水	了，	他	的
hái	zi	zhǎng	dà	le	yǐ	hòu,	dōu	bù	rèn	shi	bà
孩	子	长	大	了	以	后，	都	不	认	识	爸
ba	le									
爸	了。									

shí	duō	nián	yǐ	hòu,	dà	yǔ	zhì	shuǐ	chéng	gōng	le!
十	多	年	以	后，	大	禹	治	水	成	功	了！
dà	hé	zài	yě	bù	huì	fā	dà	shuǐ	le,	rén	men
大	河	再	也	不	会	发	大	水	了，	人	们
dōu	kuài	kuài	lè	lè	de	shēng	huó。	dà	yǔ	hái	jiāo
都	快	快	乐	乐	地	生	活。	大	禹	还	教
rén	men	zhòng	dào	zi,	yǎng	jī	yǎng	yú。	rén	men	de
人	们	种	稻	子，	养	鸡	养	鱼。	人	们	的
shēng	huó	yuè	lái	yuè	hǎo,	dà	jiā	dōu	hěn	gǎn	jī
生	活	越	来	越	好，	大	家	都	很	感	激
dà	yǔ。	zhí	dào	jīn	tiān,	rén	men	hái	cháng	cháng	gēn
大	禹。	直	到	今	天，	人	们	还	常	常	跟
hái	zi	men	shuō	dà	yǔ	zhì	shuǐ	de	gù	shì,	yào
孩	子	们	说	大	禹	治	水	的	故	事，	要
tā	men	zhǎng	dà	yǐ	hòu,	xiàng	tā	yī	yàng	rèn	zhēn
他	们	长	大	以	后，	像	他	一	样	认	真
nǔ	lì	de	gōng	zuò。						
努	力	地	工	作。						

22. KUA FU CHASES THE SUN

kuā	fù	zhuī	rì
夸	父	追	日

hěn	jiǔ	hěn	jiǔ	yǐ	qián	zài	zhōng	guó	de	běi	bù
很	久	很	久	以	前，	在	中	国	的	北	部
yǒu	yī	zuò	gāo	shān,	shān	shàng	zhù	zhe	hěn	duō	jù
有	一	座	高	山，	山	上	住	着	很	多	巨

人。他们的首领最高最大，人很
善良，也很勤劳勇敢，他的名字
叫夸父。

有一年，天气很热很热，太阳像
火一样，树木都死了，大河也干
了。很多人都热死了，渴死了。夸
父看了，心里很难过。他抬起头
看看天上的太阳说："太阳太阳，
你太坏了！我一定要追上你，把
你捉住让你听我们的话。"

人们听了，都说："你不能去呀，太
阳离我们那么远，你怎么能追
得上呢？"还有的人说："对呀，太阳
那么远又那么热，你不热死也
会累死的。"可是夸父说："为了大
家可以快乐地生活，我一定要
追上太阳！把它捉住，让它听我
们的话！"

夸父手里拿着一根木杖，往着
升起的太阳，拼命地跑。他跑过
了一片片大树林，爬过了一座
座大山，游过了一条条大河，跑
了很远很远。

就这样，夸父跑呀跑呀，离太阳
越来越近了，最后终于追上了
太阳。夸父高兴极了，他高兴地
伸出手去，想把太阳捉住。可是
太阳太热太热了，夸父捉不住，
他自己也觉得又热又渴他就
跑到河边，一口气喝干了河里
的水，又往大海跑去，想去那里
喝水，可是夸父还没有跑到大
海，就在路上渴死了。

夸父死去以前，还想着大家，所
以他把手里的木杖往太阳扔
了过去。木杖掉下来以后，变成

le	yī	dà	piàn	táo	lín,	měi	nián	shù	shàng	dōu	zhǎng
了	一	大	片	桃	林,	每	年	树	上	都	长

hěn	duō	dà	táo	zi,	gěi	guò	lù	de	rén	men	chī,
很	多	大	桃	子,	给	过	路	的	人	们	吃,

bāng	tā	men	zhǐ	kě.
帮	他	们	止	渴。

23. THE MAGIC LOTUS LAMP

bǎo lián dēng
宝 莲 灯

---

zhōng	guó	yǒu	yī	zuò	gāo	shān,	jiào	huà	shān.	hěn	jiǔ
中	国	有	一	座	高	山,	叫	华	山。	很	久

hěn	jiǔ	yǐ	qián,	shān	shàng	zhù	zhe	yī	wèi	měi	lì
很	久	以	前,	山	上	住	着	一	位	美	丽

de	nǚ	shén,	tā	de	míng	zì	jiào	sān	shèng	mǔ.	sān
的	女	神,	她	的	名	字	叫	三	圣	母。	三

shèng	mǔ	yǒu	yī	gè	bǎo	lián	dēng,	tā	cháng	cháng	yòng
圣	母	有	一	个	宝	莲	灯,	她	常	常	用

tā	lái	gěi	rén	men	kàn	bìng,	dà	jiā	dōu	hěn	gǎn
它	来	给	人	们	看	病,	大	家	都	很	感

jī	tā.
激	她。

lìng	wài	hái	yǒu	yī	gè	rén	yě	gěi	rén	men	kàn
另	外	还	有	一	个	人	也	给	人	们	看

bìng,	tā	hái	cháng	cháng	dào	huà	shān	shàng	lai	cǎi	yào.
病,	他	还	常	常	到	华	山	上	来	采	药。

tā	cǎi	yào	de	shí	hòu	rèn	shi	le	sān	shèng	mǔ,
他	采	药	的	时	候	认	识	了	三	圣	母,

tā	men	yī	qǐ	gěi	rén	men	kàn	bìng.	màn	màn	de,
他	们	一	起	给	人	们	看	病。	慢	慢	地,

tā	men	xiāng	ài	le,	jié	hūn	le.
他	们	相	爱	了,	结	婚	了。

sān	shèng	mǔ	de	gē	gē	shì	tiān	shàng	de	èr	láng
三	圣	母	的	哥	哥	是	天	上	的	二	郎

shén tā tīng shuō zì jǐ de mèi mèi hé yī gè
神，他 听 说 自 己 的 妹 妹 和 一 个

fán rén jié hūn le hěn shēng qì yī dìng yào bǎ
凡 人 结 婚 了，很 生 气，一 定 要 把

sān shèng mǔ zhuō huí qù kě shì sān shèng mǔ ná
三 圣 母 捉 回 去。可 是，三 圣 母 拿

chū tā de bǎo lián dēng bǎ tā dǎ bài le yī
出 她 的 宝 莲 灯，把 他 打 败 了。一

nián hòu sān shèng mǔ shēng le yī gè nán hái jiào
年 后，三 圣 母 生 了 一 个 男 孩，叫

chén xiāng jiù zài dà jiā gāo gāo xìng xìng de qìng
沉 香。就 在 大 家 高 高 兴 兴 地 庆

zhù de shí hòu èr láng shén jìn le sān shèng mǔ
祝 的 时 候，二 郎 神 进 了 三 圣 母

de jiā bǎ tā de bǎo lián dēng tōu zǒu le sān
的 家，把 她 的 宝 莲 灯 偷 走 了。三

shèng mǔ méi yǒu le bǎo lián dēng jiù bèi èr láng
圣 母 没 有 了 宝 莲 灯，就 被 二 郎

shén dǎ bài le yā zài le huà shān xià mian
神 打 败 了，压 在 了 华 山 下 面。

shí wǔ nián yǐ hòu xiǎo chén xiāng zhǎng dà le tā
十 五 年 以 后，小 沉 香 长 大 了，他

yòu piāo liàng yòu cōng míng bìng qiě xué le hěn duō
又 漂 亮 又 聪 明，并 且 学 了 很 多

hǎo wǔ yì
好 武 艺。

chén xiāng cháng cháng xiǎng mā ma tā shuō wǒ yī dìng
沉 香 常 常 想 妈 妈，他 说："我 一 定

yào jiù chū mā ma ràng wǒ men yī jiā tuán yuán
要 救 出 妈 妈，让 我 们 一 家 团 圆。"

yú shì tā kāi shǐ wǎng huà shān zǒu qù yǒu yī
于 是，他 开 始 往 华 山 走 去。有 一

tiān chén xiāng zài lù shàng zǒu zhe yī tiáo jù dà
天，沉 香 在 路 上 走 着，一 条 巨 大

de lóng wǎng tā fēi lái chén xiāng yī diǎn dōu bù
的 龙 往 他 飞 来。沉 香 一 点 都 不

pà tā tā gēn jù lóng dǎ qǐ lai bǎ tā zhuō
怕 它。他 跟 巨 龙 打 起 来，把 它 捉

zhù le bìng qiě bǎ tā biàn chéng le yī bǎ hěn
住 了，并 且 把 它 变 成 了 一 把 很

dà hěn cháng de fǔ zi chén xiāng gāo xìng jí le
大 很 长 的 斧 子。沉 香 高 兴 极 了，

xiào zhe shuō tài hǎo le wǒ kě yǐ yòng zhè bǎ
笑 着 说："太 好 了！我 可 以 用 这 把

fǔ zi dǎ kāi huà shān jiù chū mā ma
斧 子 打 开 华 山，救 出 妈 妈。"

chén xiāng zhōng yú zǒu dào le huà shān tā huī dòng
沉 香 终 于 走 到 了 华 山，他 挥 动

fǔ zi yòng lì pī xià qù zhǐ tīng jiàn hōng lóng
斧 子 用 力 劈 下 去，只 听 见 "轰 隆"

yī shēng huà shān bèi pī chéng le liǎng bàn chén xiāng
一 声，华 山 被 劈 成 了 两 半，沉 香

jiù chū le mā ma mā ma jiàn dào le tā gāo
救 出 了 妈 妈。妈 妈 见 到 了 他，高

xìng de yòu kū yòu xiào chén xiāng hé mā ma yòu
兴 得 又 哭 又 笑。沉 香 和 妈 妈 又

yī qǐ zhǎo dào le èr láng shén bǎ tā dǎ bài
一 起 找 到 了 二 郎 神，把 他 打 败

le ná huí le bǎo lián dēng cóng cǐ tā men yī
了，拿 回 了 宝 莲 灯。从 此，他 们 一

jiā zài yī qǐ kuài lè de shēng huó zhe tā de
家 在 一 起 快 乐 地 生 活 着，他 的

bà ba mā ma hái gēn yǐ qián yī yàng cháng cháng
爸 爸 妈 妈 还 跟 以 前 一 样，常 常

gěi dà jiā kàn bìng
给 大 家 看 病。

zhí dào jīn tiān rú guǒ nǐ qù huà shān rén men
直 到 今 天，如 果 你 去 华 山，人 们

hái huì gào su nǐ chén xiāng shì zài nǎr ér pī
还 会 告 诉 你，沉 香 是 在 哪 儿 劈

shān jiù mǔ de
山 救 母 的。

APPENDIX 2:
STORY ABSTRACTS IN ENGLISH

I: FABLES AND LITERARY QUOTATIONS

1. PULLING SEEDLINGS UP TO HELP THEM GROW

Once upon a time, there was a farmer who worked hard in the fields all year round. One spring, he got impatient with the growth of his crops. He decided to pull on the shoots in order to make them grow faster. So he doggedly pulled them, only to find all of the seedlings withered the next day. The moral of this story is that one must respect the laws of nature—excessive enthusiasm is not helpful but destructive.

2. SITTING BY A STUMP TO WAIT FOR A CARELESS HARE

Once upon a time, there was a farmer who worked hard in the fields to make ends meet. One day, he saw a hare dash over and bump into a hidden stump nearby. The poor hare died instantly. The farmer picked it up and took it home. That night, he said to himself, "I do not need to work any more. What I should do is sit by the stump and wait for a hare each day." Thus, he gave up farming and waited for more hares to bump into the stump, but it never happened again. The moral of this story is that one should not depend on a stroke of luck to achieve a goal.

3. DRAWING A SNAKE AND ADDING FEET

In ancient China, there was a wealthy man who had many servants. One day, he gave them a bottle of wine to share. Believing that one bottle of wine was not enough for so many people, the servants decided to have a drawing contest, in which the person who was the first to finish drawing a snake could have the entire bottle of wine. One man finished quickly and grabbed the bottle. Wine in hand, he saw that the other contestants were still busy drawing, and so he started to add feet to his snake. Right at that moment, another contestant finished drawing his snake. He snatched the bottle from the "winner," saying, "Snakes don't have feet. What you drew is not a snake, so the wine is mine!" The moral of this story is that one can ruin a good opportunity by attending to unnecessary, trivial details.

4. MISTAKING THE REFLECTION OF A BOW FOR A SNAKE

Once upon a time, a wealthy man named Yue Guang invited a friend for dinner. They had a good time, drinking and chatting. Suddenly, his friend pushed the wine away and rushed home. The next day, Yue Guang heard that his friend had become very ill and went to see him. When Yue Guang asked his friend why he had fallen ill, the friend said that he had seen a tiny snake in his wine while eating dinner, which gave him a severe stomachache. The next day, Yue Guang asked his friend to have a drink at the same place. The friend saw the snake in his wine again, but soon realized that it was actually the reflection of a bow hung on the wall behind him, not a snake. Immensely relieved, he immediately recovered. The moral of this story is that being overly suspicious can have terrible consequences.

5. SIX BLIND MEN AND AN ELEPHANT

In a city far, far away, there lived six blind men who were good friends and often chatted together. One day, a strange animal, called "elephant," was brought to their city. Curious, they gathered around the elephant, touching and stroking it in an attempt to figure out what it looked like. Each of the six men touched a different part of the elephant and claimed that he knew what it looked like. Unable to reach an agreement, they argued endlessly. The moral of the story is that partial knowledge is insufficient to know the truth.

6. SELF-CONTRADICTION

In ancient China, spears and shields were popular weapons for fighting battles. One day, a peddler who sold weaponry on the street lifted a spear and declared, "My spears are the sharpest in the world. They can penetrate anything." A moment later, he put down the spear and lifted a shield, saying, "My shields are the hardest in the world. Nothing can penetrate them." The peddler attracted a large crowd, and people were fascinated by the weapons. Suddenly, a man in the crowd asked, "What will happen if I use your spear to poke through your shield?" The peddler was tongue-tied, unable to answer the question. Since then, the combination of spear (矛) and shield (盾) has stood for "contradicting oneself" or "being inconsistent with oneself."

7. A FROG IN A WELL

Once upon a time, there was a little frog that was born and grew up in a well. He never traveled anywhere. Content and blissful, he felt that he was the happiest creature in the world. One day, a big sea turtle passed by. The little frog boasted to the turtle about the wideness and fineness of his well and invited the turtle to pay a visit, but the turtle could not even fit his head or foot inside. Humbled, the little frog learned from the turtle that beyond the well, there was a sea that was unfathomably large and deep. The moral of this story is that one risks being shallow and narrow-minded if one lives in a small, unchanging world.

8. THREE IN THE MORNING AND FOUR IN THE EVENING

A long time ago, there was a poor old man who lived at the foot of a mountain and befriended the monkeys living nearby. A few of the monkeys moved into his home. The old man fed them fruits. One winter, the old man had to ration their food. He first suggested to them that he would give them three fruits in the morning and four in the evening. All of the monkeys were angry and protested loudly. Then he suggested four in the morning and three in the evening. With this change, the monkeys were all satisfied and happy. This idiom originally meant "being easily fooled by small tricks," and later on it came to mean "being indecisive or unable to make up one's mind."

9. CARVING A MARK ON A BOAT TO LOOK FOR A LOST SWORD

Once upon a time, a man had a sword that he treasured dearly. One day, he went on a business trip by boat. In the middle of the river, his sword inadvertently fell into the river. His fellow passengers anxiously suggested that he jump into the water to search for it. He did not think that it was necessary. Confidently, he carved a mark on the edge of the boat where his sword had slipped off and waited until the boat reached the shore. Then he jumped into the water at the carved spot to look for his sword. The moral of this story is that one should change when circumstances change. Rigidly sticking to rules leads nowhere.

Appendix 2: Story Abstracts in English

10. AN OLD MAN ON THE FRONTIER LOSES HIS HORSE

A long time ago, there was an old man who lived on the war-ridden frontier. One day, he lost one of his horses. Everybody thought that it was a big loss, but he did not agree. It turned out that he was right, because a few months later the lost horse not only came back home but also brought a few wild horses with him. When the old man's son tried to tame one of the horses, however, he fell off and was crippled. That may have been a blessing in disguise because his son's life was saved due to the fact that he could not fight in the war. The moral of this story is that bad things may lead to good results, and good things may lead to bad outcomes.

II: SAYINGS OF IMPORTANT HISTORICAL FIGURES

11. ONE OUT OF EVERY THREE MUST BE MY MENTOR

Confucius (551–479 B.C.E.), the most well-known philosopher in China, laid the foundation of traditional Chinese culture and is one of the most influential educators and philosophers in world history. He was born in the Kingdom of Lu, which is in the present-day Shandong province. He lived in the turbulent Spring and Autumn Period (770 B.C.E.–476 B.C.E.) when China was divided into a number of small warring states. He earnestly taught the principles of maintaining social order and familial harmony, upholding morals and rituals, revering learning and education, and being a benevolent, righteous and modest person. Centuries after his death, his philosophical and educational theories are still highly respected and practiced by people all over the world. One of Confucius' educational principles is that one should be open to learning from people and surroundings. This story is about how he and his students solved a tricky problem by learning from a young girl.

12. MENCIUS' MOTHER MOVED THREE TIMES

Mencius (372–289 B.C.E.) was one of Confucius' students and, like Confucius, was a famous philosopher. He devoted his life to advocating Confucianism. He was born in the Kingdom of Zhou, which is in the present-day Shandong province, and lived during the Warring States period (475–221 B.C.E.). Following Confucius' philosophical and educational theories, he also emphasized learning, education, and rituals to cultivate good human qualities such as modesty, filial piety, and fraternal love. He believed that humans are born good-natured but are corrupted by the negative influences of society. Thus, a good education is crucial. Mencius was born into a very poor family. His mother did everything possible to secure a good education for him. To seek a better environment, she moved her family three times and finally settled in a place close to a school.

13. KONG RONG OFFERS THE BEST PEARS TO HIS BROTHERS

Kong Rong (153–208 C.E.) was a twentieth-generation descendant of Confucius who lived during the Three Kingdoms period. He was a famous Chinese politician and poet from the Kingdom of Lu, which is in the present-day Shandong province. His classical essays and poems were highly praised by his contemporaries as well as later literati. He enjoyed a fine reputation because of his character. He was even-tempered, modest, and polite, and a true follower of Confucius in practicing good manners and maintaining familial harmony. "Kong Rong Offers the Best Pears to His Brothers," a story that illustrates the Confucian ideal of fraternal love among youngsters, has been a household standard in China for centuries.

14. GRINDING DOWN AN IRON PESTLE TO A NEEDLE

Li Bai (701–762 C.E.) was a Chinese poet who lived during the Tang Dynasty (618–907 C.E.). His name traditionally was pronounced Li Bo or Li Po (depending on the romanization system), hence the familiar name Li Po by which he has long been known in the West. Called the "Poet Immortal," Li Bai is often regarded as one of the greatest poets in China's literary history. Approximately 1,100 of his poems remain today. Li Bai is best known for his vivid imagination and the striking Taoist imagery in his poetry, as well as for his great love of wine. It is said that, born into a wealthy family, young Li Bai was not studious and often skipped school. One day, when he was fooling around, he bumped into an elderly woman who was grinding an iron pestle into a needle. He was immensely moved by her perseverance and thereafter became a diligent pupil.

15. BRINGING A BIRCH AND BEGGING FOR A FLOGGING

Lian Po (廉颇), a general, and Lin Xiangru (蔺相如), a statesman, were both prominent officials of the State of Zhao (赵国) during the Warring States period in China. Thanks to his superb grasp of the art of war, Lian Po rarely lost a battle and hence became a very respected general. However, Lin Xiangru also rendered outstanding service to the Emperor and was promoted above Lian Po. Lian Po was so angry that he announced he would humiliate Lin Xiangru the next time they met. Lin Xiangru decided to avoid Lian Po and avert a conflict. Later on, Lian Po realized his mistake and went to Lin Xiangru's house, carrying a birch on his naked back, and asked for punishment for his wrongdoing. This idiom illustrates the courage it takes to confess one's mistakes and offer a sincere apology.

16. CAO CHONG WEIGHS AN ELEPHANT

Cao Chong (曹冲) (196–208 C.E.) was a son of Cao Cao (曹操), a powerful Chinese warlord, politician, and poet who lived during the Three Kingdoms (三国) period (220–280 C.E.). Cao Chong was renowned as a child prodigy and was said to have a mature intelligence by the age of five. Among Chinese people, he is most well known today for his ingenious method of weighing an elephant using the law of buoyancy. The story is told like this: One day, the powerful Cao Cao was given a big elephant. Wondering how much the elephant weighed, Cao Cao asked his subordinates if they could find out. None of them could because they had no scale to weigh such a big animal. Then little five-year-old Cao Chong came forward and successfully solved the problem. First, he put the elephant into a boat. He marked the water level on the side of the boat. After the elephant was removed, he filled up the boat with stones until it sank an equal depth into the water. Finally, by weighing the stones, Cao Chong found out the weight of the elephant.

17. BREAKING THE WATER VAT TO SAVE A LIFE

Sima Guang (司马光) (1019–1086 C.E.) was a Chinese historian, scholar, and statesman of the Song dynasty (960–1279 C.E.) in ancient China. He was born to a wealthy family and obtained early success as a scholar and an official. He passed the highest scholarly examination in the state when he was barely twenty. Today he is still remembered for his great historical work, *Comprehensive Mirror to Aid in Government* (资治通鉴). Sima

Guang showed outstanding talent at a very early age. One of the most famous stories about him is that when he was seven years old, he forcefully broke a large vat full of water to rescue his playmate, who had accidentally fallen in.

III: MYTHS AND FANTASIES

18. BIRD JINGWEI FILLS UP THE SEA

In Chinese mythology, the Yan Emperor, Yandi (炎帝), was a legendary hero believed to have taught his people how to cultivate grains for food. It is said that he had a beautiful daughter whose name was Nuwa (女娃). One day when Nuwa was in a boat on the sea, she was caught in a big storm and drowned. Yandi was heartbroken and mourned for his lost daughter every day. Meanwhile, Nuwa's spirit transformed into a lovely bird, called Jingwei (精卫). Bird Jingwei hated the sea and decided to fill it up to keep other people from drowning. She flew back and forth tirelessly, finding pebbles and branches and throwing them into the sea. The sea laughed at her, saying that it would take her ten thousand years to fill it up. Brave and diligent, Jingwei never stopped. The Chinese people appreciate the story and use "Jingwei tian hai" (精卫填海) as an expression of perseverance and determination.

19. GODDESS NUWA MENDS THE SKY

In ancient China, there was a kind and beautiful goddess named Nuwa. She created her people and taught them the secrets of marriage and childbirth. One day, the heavens collapsed, fires burned out of control, waters flooded the land, and people became ill and died. To save the universe and her people, the Goddess Nuwa made a paste of colorful stones to mend the sky and used the feet of the Great Turtle as poles to support it. Thanks to Nuwa's efforts, the universe and its people returned to normal. However, Nuwa had worked so hard that she became sick and died. Her people mourned and everlastingly worshiped her as their beautiful beloved goddess.

Appendix 2: Story Abstracts in English

20. PANGU CREATES THE UNIVERSE

In Chinese mythology, Pangu (盘古) was a hero who created the universe by separating the sky (the Yang) from the earth (the Yin). It is said that, in the beginning, there was nothing but formless chaos. Out of the chaos, Pangu was conceived in an egg, where he slept for eighteen thousand years until one day he woke up and broke the egg open with a giant axe. The clear and light part of the broken egg rose up and became the sky, while the murky and heavy part of the broken egg sank and became the earth. Pangu stood between them and grew ten feet taller each day, which pushed the sky ten feet higher and the earth ten feet lower. As the sky became higher and higher, the earth became thicker and thicker. At the end of another eighteen thousand years, the sky was very high, the earth was very thick, and Pangu lay down to rest. After his death, Pangu's body turned into huge mountains, his blood formed great rivers, and his hair became flowers, grass, and trees.

21. DA YU CONTROLS THE GREAT FLOOD

Stories that depict a period known as the Great Flood appear in Chinese mythology, just as they do in the Sumerian and Greek traditions. During the Chinese Great Flood, a ruler called Da Yu (大禹, "The Great Yu") arose. Da Yu was an extremely moral and benevolent ruler, and with the help of the Goddess Nuwa, he organized his people to dig canals and build irrigation systems. He finally controlled the floods and taught his people to grow crops and raise poultry. In order to control the great floods, he worked so hard and so diligently that he did not visit his family for decades, and his children grew up without knowing him. He is said to have passed his own house three times without stopping once. Thus, Da Yu is held in high regard as an example of integrity and discipline, and the expression "Da Yu zhi shui" (大禹治水) stands for diligence and perseverance.

22. KUA FU CHASES THE SUN

Kua Fu (夸父) was a kind and brave giant in Chinese mythology. He lived with his fellow giants in a remote mountainous area. One year, the sun was extraordinarily hot; trees and plants withered, rivers dried up, and many people died. Kua Fu was baffled, and decided to chase and catch the sun. Wooden club in hand, he followed the sun from the East to the West; however, he could not finish his quest because the sun was too hot. Kua Fu succumbed to extreme heat and exhaustion, but before his death, he gathered all his strength and threw the wooden club toward the sun. The club grew into a vast peach orchard, which helped passersby to quench their thirst. Although he did not reach his goal, Kua Fu is praised as a symbol of determination and courage.

23. THE MAGIC LOTUS LAMP

In Chinese mythology, there was a beautiful goddess who lived in Mount Hua and was called San Sheng Mu (三圣母), the Holy Mother of Mount Hua. She had a magic lotus lamp, which she often used to treat disease. During her medical practice, she fell in love with a man who often climbed Mount Hua to gather medicinal herbs for his patients. They got married and had a son called Chen Xiang (沉香). However, San Sheng Mu's brother, Er-lang Shen (二郎神), was angry because she had married a mortal. He captured San Sheng Mu and pinned her under Mount Hua. Fifteen years later, the couple's son, Chen Xiang, grew up to be a brave young man with marvelous skill in the martial arts. He set out to rescue his mother. On his way to Mount Hua, he encountered a flying dragon. He captured it and turned it into a giant axe, with which he broke up Mount Hua and successfully rescued his mother. His family was reunited, and they lived happily ever after.

Appendix 2: Story Abstracts in English

VOCABULARY INDEX

生词索引
生詞索引

SIMPLIFIED	TRADITIONAL	*PINYIN*	PART OF SPEECH	ENGLISH	STORY NUMBER
A					
安慰	安慰	ānwèi	v.	to comfort	10
B					
拔	拔	bá	v.	to pull	1
包	包	bāo	v.	to envelop	20
宝	寶	bǎo	n.	valuable	9
保护	保護	bǎohù	v.	to protect	6
宝莲灯	寶蓮燈	Bǎolián dēng	pn.	magic lotus lamp	23
报仇	報仇	bào chóu	vo.	to avenge	18
杯	杯	bēi	n.	cup	4
背	背	bèi	v.	to carry on one's back	15
鼻子	鼻子	bízi	n.	nose (in this story, an elephant's trunk)	5
比赛	比賽	bǐsài	v.	competition	3
边	邊	biān	n.	edge, seashore	7
边境	邊境	biānjìng	n.	border	10
变	變	biàn	v.	to change, to transform	18, 19, 20, 22, 23
并且	並且	bìngqiě	conj.	also	2, 4, 23

SIMPLIFIED	TRADITIONAL	*PINYIN*	PART OF SPEECH	ENGLISH	STORY NUMBER
不论	不論	búlùn	conj.	no matter	6
补	補	bǔ	v.	to mend	19
部分	部分	bùfen	n.	part, portion	5
不和	不和	bùhé	adj.	to not get along	15

C

踩	踩	cǎi	v.	to step on	20
采药	採藥	cǎiyào	v.	to gather herbs	23
残疾	殘疾	cánjí	n.	disability	10
曹操	曹操	Cáo Cāo	pn.	name of a person	16
草	草	cǎo	n.	grass	10
长处	長處	chángchù	n.	strong points	11
场	場	chǎng	mw.	measure word for happenings or occurrences	3
沉	沉	chén	v.	to sink	16, 17
沉香	沉香	Chén Xiāng	pn.	name of a person	23
称	稱	chēng	v.	to scale	16
成功	成功	chénggōng	v.	to succeed	14, 18, 21
城市	城市	chéngshì	n.	city	5
秤	秤	chèng	n.	scale	16
虫	蟲	chóng	n.	insect, worm	7
仇恨	仇恨	chóuhèn	v.	to hate	18
穿过	穿過	chuānguo	vc.	to pass through	11
船	船	chuán	n.	boat	9, 16, 18
传说	傳說	chuánshuō	n.	legend	18, 19, 21
创造	創造	chuàngzào	v.	to create	19
吹牛	吹牛	chuī niú	vo.	to brag	7

SIMPLIFIED	TRADITIONAL	*PINYIN*	PART OF SPEECH	ENGLISH	STORY NUMBER
刺穿	刺穿	cìchuān	v.	to poke through	6
从此	從此	cóngcǐ	conj.	thereupon	14, 18, 23
粗	粗	cū	adj.	thick and strong	5, 14, 15
村子	村子	cūnzi	n.	village	1, 10

D

打败	打敗	dǎbài	vc.	to defeat	23
打动	打動	dǎdòng	vc.	to be moved	14
打翻	打翻	dǎfān	v.	to be capsized	18
打仗	打仗	dǎzhàng	v.	to fight, to be at war	6, 10
大叫	大叫	dàjiào	v.	to yell	4, 14
代	代	dài	n.	generation	4, 13
待	待	dài	v.	to wait	2
当然	當然	dāngrán	adv.	surely	10, 15
挡住	擋住	dǎngzhù	v.	to block	6
刀	刀	dāo	n.	knife, dagger	9
道歉	道歉	dàoqiàn	v.	to apologize	15
稻子	稻子	dàozi	n.	rice, paddy	21
底	底	dǐ	n.	bottom	7
点头	點頭	diǎntóu	v.	to nod one's head	8
掉	掉	diào	v.	to drop, to fall	4, 9, 10, 17, 20, 22
顶	頂	dǐng	v.	to prop up, to push up	20
丢	丢	diū	v.	to lose	10
东海	東海	dōnghǎi	pn.	the East Sea	7
懂	懂	dǒng	v.	to understand	8
洞	洞	dòng	n.	hole	19

SIMPLIFIED	TRADITIONAL	*PINYIN*	PART OF SPEECH	ENGLISH	STORY NUMBER
堵	堵	dǔ	mw.	measure word for walls	5
短	短	duǎn	adj.	short	5
对岸	對岸	duì'àn	n.	the opposite shore	9
对立	對立	duìlì	n.	to oppose	6
盾	盾	dùn	n.	shield	6
多重	多重	duōzhòng	n.	how heavy…?	16
躲	躲	duǒ	v.	to hide, to avoid	15

E

恶心	噁心	ěxīn	v.	to feel sick	4
耳朵	耳朵	ěrduō	n.	ear	5
二郎神	二郎神	Èr Láng Shén	pn.	name of a god	23

F

凡人	凡人	fánrén	n.	mortal	23
方圆	方圓	fāngyuán	n.	circumference	7
防卫	防衛	fángwèi	v.	to protect oneself	6
房子	房子	fángzi	n.	house	21
分成	分成	fēnchéng	vc.	to be divided into	6
锋利	鋒利	fēnglì	adj.	sharp	6
浮	浮	fú	v.	to float	16
抚养	撫養	fúyǎng	v.	to raise	12
斧子	斧子	fǔzi	n.	axe, hatchet	20, 23
负荆	負荊	fù jīng	vo.	to carry a birch	15
富人	富人	fùrén	n.	rich person	3

SIMPLIFIED	TRADITIONAL	*PINYIN*	PART OF SPEECH	ENGLISH	STORY NUMBER
G					
感动	感動	gǎndòng	v.	to be moved, to be touched	19
感激	感激	gǎnjī	v.	to feel grateful	17, 19, 20, 21, 23
赶快	趕快	gǎnkuài	adv.	quickly	9, 11, 15, 17
缸	缸	gāng	n.	vat	17
根	根	gēn	mw.	measure word for long, slender objects	15, 18, 22
根本	根本	gēnběn	adv.	actually	4
弓	弓	gōng	n.	bow	4
功劳	功勞	gōngláo	n.	meritorious service	15
挂	掛	guà	v.	to hang	4
官	官	guān	n.	government official	15, 16
管子	管子	guǎnzi	n.	tube	5
光滑	光滑	guānghuá	adj.	smooth	5
国王	國王	guówáng	n.	king	11, 15
果子	果子	guǒzi	n.	fruit	8
过错	過錯	guòcuò	n.	fault, mistake	3
H					
海	海	hǎi	n.	sea	7, 18, 22
海龟	海龜	hǎigūi	n.	sea turtle	7
海浪	海浪	hǎilàng	n.	sea waves	18
喊	喊	hǎn	v.	to scream	17
汗	汗	hàn	n.	sweat	14

SIMPLIFIED	TRADITIONAL	*PINYIN*	PART OF SPEECH	ENGLISH	STORY NUMBER
合	合	hé	v.	to join, to combine	20
禾苗	禾苗	hémiáo	n.	shoots of grain	1
轰隆	轟隆	hōnglōng	on.	the sound of rumbling	23
猴子	猴子	hóuzi	n.	monkey	8
花草	花草	huācǎo	n.	flowers and grass	20
画	畫	huà	v./n.	to draw, painting	3
坏	壞	huài	adj.	bad, vicious	10
环境	環境	huánjìng	n.	environment	12
挥动	揮動	huīdòng	v.	to brandish	20, 23
昏	昏	hūn	v.	to faint	2
活	活	huó	v.	to be alive	10
火神	火神	huǒshén	n.	the god of fire	19

J

鸡蛋	雞蛋	jīdàn	n.	egg	20
急急忙忙	急急忙忙	jíjímáng-máng	adj.	in a hurry	4
记号	記號	jìhào	n.	mark	9, 16
坚强	堅強	jiānqiáng	adj.	strong	18
坚硬	堅硬	jiānyìng	adj.	hard, strong	6
简单	簡單	jiǎndān	adj.	simple	16
剑	劍	jiàn	n.	sword	9
健康的	健康的	jiànkāng de	adj.	healthy	10
浆	漿	jiāng	n.	thick liquid, paste	19
将军	將軍	jiāngjūn	n.	military general	15
江心	江心	jiāngxīn	n.	middle of the river	9
骄傲	驕傲	jiāo'ào	adj.	arrogant, proud	15
浇水	澆水	jiāo shǔi	vo.	to give water to plants	1

SIMPLIFIED	TRADITIONAL	*PINYIN*	PART OF SPEECH	ENGLISH	STORY NUMBER
脚	腳	jiǎo	n.	foot	3, 7, 19, 20
教育	教育	jiàoyù	n./v.	education, to educate	12
接近	接近	jiējìn	v.	to be around	12
接受	接受	jiēshòu	v.	to receive	12
结婚	結婚	jié hūn	vo.	to get married	19, 23
金属	金屬	jīnshǔ	n.	metal	6
进攻	進攻	jìngōng	v.	to attack	6, 15
井	井	jǐng	n.	well	7
井台	井臺	jǐngtái	n.	the mouth of a well	7
救	救	jiù	v.	to rescue	17, 23
巨人	巨人	jùrén	n.	giant	22

K

SIMPLIFIED	TRADITIONAL	*PINYIN*	PART OF SPEECH	ENGLISH	STORY NUMBER
考察	考察	kǎochá	v.	to inspect	21
可怕	可怕	kěpà	adj.	terrifying	15
可惜	可惜	kěxī	adj.	pitiful	9, 10
刻	刻	kè	v.	to carve	9
孔融	孔融	Kǒng Róng	pn.	a descendant of Confucius	13
孔子	孔子	Kǒngzǐ	pn.	Confucius	11, 12, 13
哭	哭	kū	v.	to cry	12, 17, 18, 23
夸	誇	kuā	v.	to praise	13
块	塊	kuài	mw.	measure word for a piece, lump, chunk	2, 14, 17
快乐	快樂	kuàilè	adj.	happy	7, 19, 21, 22, 23

SIMPLIFIED	TRADITIONAL	*PINYIN*	PART OF SPEECH	ENGLISH	STORY NUMBER
矛	矛	máo	n.	spear	6
毛发	毛髮	máofà	n.	hair	20
矛头	矛頭	máotóu	n.	spearhead	6
美丽	美麗	měilì	adj.	beautiful	19, 20, 23
孟子	孟子	Mèngzǐ	pn.	Mencius	12
面	面	miàn	mw.	measure word for mirrors, flags, etc.	6
苗	苗	miáo	n.	seedling, shoot	1
摸	摸	mō	v.	to touch, to feel	5, 20
磨	磨	mó	v.	to grind	14
暮	暮	mù	n.	evening	8
木柄	木柄	mùbǐng	n.	wooden handle	6
墓地	墓地	mùdì	adj.	cemetery	12
木杖	木杖	mùzhàng	n.	cane, stick	22
N					
难过	難過	nánguò	adj.	sad, heartbroken	22
年纪	年紀	niánjì	n.	age	13, 16, 17
年轻人	年輕人	niánqīngrén	n.	young man	9
鸟	鳥	niǎo	n.	bird	18
农民	農民	nóngmín	n.	farmer	1, 2
女神	女神	nǚshén	n.	goddess	19, 23
女娲	女娲	Nǚwá	pn.	name of a person	18
P					
爬	爬	pá	v.	to crawl	11, 17, 22
佩服	佩服	pèifu	v.	to admire	17, 18

SIMPLIFIED	TRADITIONAL	*PINYIN*	PART OF SPEECH	ENGLISH	STORY NUMBER
喷	噴	pēn	v.	to gush	19
砰	砰	pēng	on.	the sound of a bang	17, 20
劈	劈	pī	v.	to cleave, to split	23
匹	匹	pǐ	mw.	measure word for horses	10
拼命地	拼命地	pīnmìng de	adv.	defying death	22
平	平	píng	v.	to fill up	18
破	破	pò	v./adj.	to break, broken	17, 19
仆人	僕人	púrén	n.	servant	3, 15

Q

妻子	妻子	qīzi	n.	wife	21
齐	齊	qí	v.	to be on a level with	16
奇怪	奇怪	qíguài	adj.	strange, surprised	4, 13, 14
牵	牽	qiān	v.	to lead along	16
墙	牆	qiáng	n.	wall	4, 5
抢	搶	qiǎng	v.	to grab	3
勤劳	勤勞	qínláo	adj.	hard-working	22
轻	輕	qīng	adj.	light	20
情况	情況	qíngkuàng	n.	situation, condition	6, 21
请罪	請罪	qǐng zuì	vo.	to ask for punishment	15
穷	窮	qióng	adj.	poor	12
求	求	qiú	v.	to look for	9
全	全	quán	adv.	entire	5

R

认真	認真	rènzhēn	adv.	seriously, diligently	14, 21
扔	扔	rēng	v.	to throw, to toss	22

SIMPLIFIED	TRADITIONAL	*PINYIN*	PART OF SPEECH	ENGLISH	STORY NUMBER
S					
塞	塞	sài	n.	border, frontier	10
塞翁	塞翁	Sàiwēng	pn.	name of a person	10
三圣母	三聖母	Sān Shèngmǔ	pn.	Holy Mother of Mount Hua	23
晒	曬	shài	v.	to sunbathe	7
搧	搧	shān	v.	to wave a fan	5
善良	善良	shànliáng	adj.	kind-hearted	19, 22
扇子	扇子	shànzi	n.	fan	5
伤心	傷心	shāngxīn	adj.	heartbroken	10, 18, 19
蛇	蛇	shé	n.	snake	3, 4
伸	伸	shēn	v.	to reach out	7, 13, 22
深	深	shēn	adj.	deep	7, 17
深深地	深深地	shēnshen de	adv.	deeply	14
身体	身體	shēntǐ	n.	body	5, 6, 7, 20
升	升	shēng	v.	to lift	20, 22
生活	生活	shēnghuó	v.	to live	7, 19, 21, 22, 23
生气	生氣	shēngqì	adj.	angry	3, 12, 15, 23
绳子	繩子	shéngzi	n.	rope	5
省	省	shěng	v.	to save	8
胜仗	勝仗	shèng zhàng	n.	triumphant battles	15
失	失	shī	v.	to lose	10
诗	詩	shī	n.	poem	14
诗人	詩人	shīrén	n.	poet	14
拾	拾	shí	v.	to pick up	2

SIMPLIFIED	TRADITIONAL	*PINYIN*	PART OF SPEECH	ENGLISH	STORY NUMBER
石头	石頭	shítou	n.	stone	14, 16, 17, 18
市场	市場	shìchǎng	n.	market	6
适合	適合	shìhé	adj.	suitable	12
世界	世界	shìjiè	n.	world	7
守	守	shǒu	v.	to stay around	2
首领	首領	shǒulǐng	n.	leader	22
受伤	受傷	shòu shāng	vo.	to be injured	10
熟悉	熟悉	shúxī	v.	to get familiar with	8
树木	樹木	shùmù	n.	trees	20, 22
树枝	樹枝	shùzhī	n.	tree branch	18
树桩	樹樁	shùzhuāng	n.	tree stump	2
拴	拴	shuān	v.	to tie	11
水面	水面	shuǐmiàn	n.	the water's surface	16
水神	水神	shuǐshén	n.	the god of water	19
说明	說明	shūomíng	v.	to show	12, 14
思想家	思想家	sīxiǎngjiā	n.	philosopher, thinker	11, 12, 13
死	死	sǐ	v.	to die or to become withered	1, 10, 12, 19, 20, 22
算	算	suàn	v.	to calculate	8

T

塌	塌	tā	v.	to fall	19, 21
抬	抬	tái	v.	to lift	4, 14, 22
桃林	桃林	táolín	n.	peach orchard	22
逃学	逃學	táo xué	vo.	to play truant	14
讨论	討論	tǎolùn	v.	to discuss	21

SIMPLIFIED	TRADITIONAL	*PINYIN*	PART OF SPEECH	ENGLISH	STORY NUMBER
特别	特别	tèbié	adv.	specially	10, 17
天	天	tiān	n.	sky	19
添	添	tiān	v.	to add	3
填平	填平	tiánpíng	vc.	to be filled up	11, 19
跳	跳	tiào	v.	to jump	7, 8, 9
铁杵	鐵杵	tiě chǔ	n.	iron pestle	14
停	停	tíng	v.	to stop	18, 19, 21
同意	同意	tóngyì	v.	to agree	8
偷走	偷走	tōuzǒu	vc.	to steal	23
投	投	tóu	v.	to throw	18
兔	兔	tù	n.	hare, rabbit	2
团圆	團圓	tuányuán	n.	reunion	23
推开	推開	tuīkāi	v.	to push away	4
腿	腿	tuǐ	n.	leg	5, 21

W

蛙	蛙	wā	n.	frog	7
弯弯曲曲	彎彎曲曲	wānwānqūqū	adj.	crooked	11
围	圍	wéi	v.	to surround	16
尾巴	尾巴	wěibā	n.	tail	5
翁	翁	wēng	n.	elderly man	10
武器	武器	wǔqì	n.	weapon	6
武艺	武藝	wǔyì	n.	martial arts	23

X

吓	嚇	xià	v.	to be scared	4
线	線	xiàn	n.	thread	11

SIMPLIFIED	TRADITIONAL	*PINYIN*	PART OF SPEECH	ENGLISH	STORY NUMBER
香	香	xiāng	adj.	fragrant, sweet-smelling	3
相	相	xiāng	adv.	each other	6, 8, 16, 23
象	象	xiàng	n.	elephant	5, 16
小孔	小孔	xiǎokǒng	n.	small holes	11
笑话	笑話	xiàohuà	n.	joke, laughingstock	2
辛辛苦苦	辛辛苦苦	xīnxīnkǔkǔ	adj.	painstaking	2
星	星	xīng	n.	star	7
行	行	xíng	v.	to walk	11
醒	醒	xǐng	v.	to wake up	20
休息	休息	xiūxi	v.	to rest	2, 7, 8
血液	血液	xuèyè	n.	blood	20
驯服	馴服	xùnfú	v.	to tame	10
Y					
牙齿	牙齒	yáchǐ	n.	teeth (elephant's tusk)	5
淹死	淹死	yānsǐ	v.	to be drowned	18, 21
炎帝	炎帝	Yándì	pn.	Yan Emperor (Yandi)	18
研究	研究	yánjiū	v.	to study, to research	21
摇头	搖頭	yáotóu	v.	to shake one's head	7, 8
野草	野草	yěcǎo	n.	weeds, wild grass	2
野马	野馬	yěmǎ	n.	wild horse	10
意见	意見	yìjiàn	n.	opinion	8
毅力	毅力	yìlì	n.	perseverance	18
英雄	英雄	yīngxióng	n.	hero	20
影	影	yǐng	n.	reflection	4

SIMPLIFIED	TRADITIONAL	*PINYIN*	PART OF SPEECH	ENGLISH	STORY NUMBER
影响	影響	yǐngxiǎng	v.	to affect	21
映	映	yìng	v.	to reflect	4
勇敢	勇敢	yǒnggǎn	adj.	brave	17, 22
永远	永遠	yǒngyuǎn	adv.	everlastingly	19, 20
优美	優美	yōuměi	adj.	beautiful, elegant	14
有名	有名	yǒumíng	adj.	famous	11, 12, 13, 17
于是	於是	yúshì	conj.	therefore	23
宇宙	宇宙	yǔzhòu	n.	universe, cosmos	20
圆	圓	yuán	adj.	round	5
乐广	樂廣	Yuè Guǎng	pn.	name of a person	4

Z

SIMPLIFIED	TRADITIONAL	*PINYIN*	PART OF SPEECH	ENGLISH	STORY NUMBER
砸	砸	zá	v.	to break with force	17
增厚	增厚	zēnghòu	vc.	to become thick	20
战争	戰爭	zhànzhēng	n.	war	10
长	長	zhǎng	v.	to grow	1
丈	丈	zhàng	mw.	a unit of length equal to 3 1/3 meters	1, 2, 12, 20, 21, 22, 23
朝	朝	zhāo	n.	morning	8
着急	著急	zháojí	adj.	to be anxious	1, 9, 19
赵国	趙國	Zhào Guó	pn.	State of Zhao	15
针	針	zhēn	n.	needle	14
之	之	zhī	part.	indicates possession	7
只	只	zhī	mw.	measure word for animals	2, 5, 7, 8, 11, 16, 18
枝	枝	zhī	mw.	measure word for a spear	6

SIMPLIFIED	TRADITIONAL	PINYIN	PART OF SPEECH	ENGLISH	STORY NUMBER
支撑	支撑	zhīchēng	v.	to prop up	19, 20
止	止	zhǐ	v.	to stop	22
治水	治水	zhì shuǐ	vo.	to control the flood	21
终于	終於	zhōngyú	adv.	finally	22, 23
肿	腫	zhǒng	adj.	swollen	21
种子	種子	zhǒngzi	n.	seeds	1
重量	重量	zhòngliàng	n.	weight	16
舟	舟	zhōu	n.	boat	9
株	株	zhū	n.	tree stump	2
珠子	珠子	zhūzi	n.	beads	11
注意	注意	zhùyì	v.	to pay attention to	12
柱子	柱子	zhùzi	n.	pillar	5
专心	專心	zhuānxīn	adj.	wholly absorbed	17
装满	裝滿	zhuāngmǎn	vc.	to be fully loaded	17
撞	撞	zhuàng	v.	to collide	2
追	追	zhuī	v.	to chase	22
准备	準備	zhǔnbèi	v.	to prepare	8,
捉迷藏	捉迷藏	zhuō mícáng	v.	to play hide-and-seek	17
捉住	捉住	zhuōzhù	vc.	to be caught, to grasp	17, 22, 23
子孙	子孫	zǐsūn	n.	descendant	13
仔细	仔細	zǐxì	n.	carefully	2
自	自	zì	n.	self	3, 4, 5, 6, 7, 8, 9, 10, 15, 17, 20, 21, 22, 23
足	足	zú	n.	feet	3
座	座	zuò	mw.	measure word for mountains	8

ANSWER KEY

(READING COMPREHENSION ONLY)

Story 1
1. C
2. A
3. D
4. C
5. A
6. B
7. D

Story 2
1. B
2. D
3. B
4. C
5. D
6. C
7. C

Story 3
1. B
2. D
3. C
4. C
5. A
6. D
7. A

Story 4
1. C
2. D
3. B
4. C
5. B
6. D
7. B

Story 5
1. D
2. A
3. C
4. B
5. C
6. C
7. B

Story 6
1. B
2. C
3. D
4. D
5. A
6. D
7. B

Story 7

1. D
2. B
3. B
4. C
5. D
6. C
7. A

Story 9

1. D
2. B
3. A
4. C
5. B
6. B
7. D

Story 11

1. B
2. B
3. C
4. B
5. D
6. C
7. D

Story 8

1. D
2. B
3. C
4. A
5. D
6. B
7. D

Story 10

1. D
2. A
3. B
4. C
5. D
6. D
7. C

Story 12

1. C
2. B
3. C
4. D
5. A
6. D
7. A

Story 13
1. C
2. C
3. B
4. A
5. B
6. D
7. D

Story 14
1. A
2. D
3. C
4. B
5. C
6. B
7. D

Story 15
1. A
2. B
3. A
4. C
5. C
6. D
7. D

Story 16
1. B
2. D
3. A
4. C
5. B
6. C
7. B

Story 17
1. C
2. B
3. D
4. C
5. D
6. B
7. A

Story 18
1. C
2. D
3. D
4. A
5. B
6. D
7. D

Story 19

1. A
2. B
3. A
4. B
5. D
6. C
7. C

Story 20

1. C
2. B
3. A
4. D
5. A
6. C
7. B

Story 21

1. D
2. B
3. D
4. C
5. D
6. A
7. B

Story 22

1. D
2. C
3. A
4. D
5. A
6. B
7. C

Story 23

1. B
2. C
3. D
4. A
5. A
6. C
7. C

ABOUT THE AUTHORS

Yun Xiao is Professor of Chinese Language and Linguistics at Bryant University. She has a Ph.D. degree in linguistics. Her research interests are second language acquisition and pedagogy, Chinese syntax and discourse analysis, and Chinese teacher education. Her recent publications include more than twenty articles and book chapters. She is the primary author of *Tales and Traditions* (Volumes 1–4, 2007–2010); co-author/ co-editor of *Chinese as a Heritage Language: Fostering Rooted World Citizenry* (2008); co-author/co-editor of *Chinese as a Foreign Language: Theories and Applications* (2009); and primary editor of *Current Issues in Chinese Linguistics* (2011).

Faye Hui Xiao is Associate Professor in the Department of East Asian Languages and Cultures at the University of Kansas. Her special areas of interest include modern and contemporary Chinese literature, popular culture, film studies, and gender studies. Her publications have appeared in *Asian Cinema, Journal of Contemporary China, Chinese Films in Focus (2nd edition), Globalization and Chineseness: Postcolonial Readings of Contemporary Culture,* and *From Camera Lens to Critical Lens: A Collection of Best Essays on Film Adaptation.* She is the author of *Family Revolution: Marital Strife in Contemporary Chinese Literature and Visual Culture* (2014) and a co-author of Volumes 1, 2, and 4 of *Tales and Traditions.*

Ying Wang is a Visiting Instructor of Chinese at Wheaton College. She obtained her M.A. from the Department of Asian Languages and Literatures at the University of Massachusetts Amherst and her B.A. in Chinese Language and Literature from Beijing University. She has taught at the Central Broadcasting and TV University in Beijing. Her areas of interest include classical Chinese literature; the history of Chinese writing; and the development, simplification, and standardization of Chinese characters. She is the author of *The Selected Works of Chinese Classical Literature,* and translator of two books for children by Chiang Yee: *Chin-Pao at the Zoo* and *Chin-Pao and the Giant Pandas.*

FOR FURTHER STUDY

More Readers Published by Cheng & Tsui

Readings in Chinese Culture Series, Volumes 1–5
By Weijia Huang, Qun Ao

Increase reading and cultural proficiency with original, level-appropriate essays about ancient and contemporary Chinese culture.

1: The Sky Is Bright with Stars	978-0-88727-818-1
2: How Far Away Is the Sun?	978-0-88727-535-7
3: The Moon Is Always Beautiful	978-0-88727-637-8
4: Where Does the Wind Blow?	978-0-88727-881-5
5: Watching the Clouds Go By	978-1-62291-055-7

Chinese Biographies Series, Second Edition

By Grace Wu

Readings in natural, authentic language chronicle the lives of modern-day, Chinese-speaking pop culture icons. Available in simplified characters.

	With *pinyin* annotations	Without *pinyin* annotations
Lang Lang	978-1-62291-098-4	978-1-62291-100-4
Yao Ming	978-1-62291-097-7	978-1-62291-099-1
Jay Chou	978-1-62291-109-7	978-1-62291-110-3
Jeremy Lin	978-1-62291-111-0	978-1-62291-112-7
Ang Lee	978-1-62291-113-4	978-1-62291-114-1
Vera Wang	978-1-62291-107-3	978-1-62291-108-0

Reference Texts Published by Cheng & Tsui

The Way of Chinese Characters, Second Edition
The Origins of 670 Essential Words
漢字之道

By Jianshin Wu, Illustrated by Chen Zheng and Chen Tian

Enrich character study with cultural insight, linguistic context, and playful illustrations.

978-1-62291-046-5

Cheng & Tsui Chinese Character Dictionary
A Guide to the 2000 Most Frequently Used Characters
剑桥学生写字字典

Edited by Wang Huidi

Carry this pocket-sized guide of 2,000 core characters organized alphabetically by *pinyin* to reference stroke orders, basic meaning, and examples of use.

978-0-88727-314-8